CHAPTER ONE

Attitude, Actions, Relations and Pressure

One project manager that I know, just announced his resignation. A short project with difficult and extremely standardized procedures, and the foreseen risk of failure, seem to be the main reasons. And, no, this will not be one of the case studies. I will use many others, but not this particular one. This is just a starting point for my, maybe counter-intuitive at this point, claim that performance under pressure is not only possible, but easy.

And, there are three simple strategies:

1. develop the right attitude for performance under pressure,

2. take action for performance under pressure, and

3. achieve relational performance under pressure.

These strategies would maybe have prevented the above mentioned manager to resign, and would have been decisive in helping yet another project to be successful. Why? The answer is old and simple, but sometime bad behaviors and attitudes need to be replaced and this takes time and effort. A positive attitude, strong action skills and great relationships will help you manage pressure and achieve the results that are expected from you.

I am not claiming this to be an extraordinary discovery, I'm here to tell again an old story. One that we tend to forget. No, we are not the only person under pressure, and some deal with success with it. I'll just remind you how these not at all amazing people do it. So, in the next chapters, I invite you to discover the simple recipe for achieving performance under pressure.

Pressure can be for some energizing or invigorating, but for most of us and without proper management it can cause excessive stress. Too much stress can lead to diminished focus, impaired judgment, and reduced ability to perform under pressure. And, you know all too well that this happens. Causes of pressure vary between individuals but there are four factors that are common causes of pressure in the workplace: time pressure, work overload, relationship strain, and having to balance competing interests.

Pressure can be a force that helps you achieve amazing results. You have for sure heard people saying that they work well under pressure. And, this is — up to a point — true and desirable. But, on the other hand, pressure can be debilitating and hinder your ability to perform when it causes excessive stress. We are humans and we function like this.

To understand your response to stress — a good starting point, you need to consider who you are — your attitudes and values, your personality, your past experiences, and your preferences. And you also need to learn to recognize potential symptoms of stress — physical, emotional, cognitive, and behavioral. To put it simply, you need to recognize pressure, its effects, and your reaction in such situation.

It's also important to realize the different ways that stress can impair your work performance by negatively impacting on your creativity, decision-making, emotions, and interpersonal skills. Developing the right attitude while under pressure can help you to optimize your performance, increase your energy levels, recognize opportunities, and respond creatively to challenges. But, you know that under pressure this is sometime difficult.

There are **two main principles to help you control your reaction to pressure**. First, you take control of yourself by taking stock of your emotions, establishing a sense of calm, accepting that you can't control everything, and using self-talk. Second, you cultivate a "success mentality" by using your emotions to your advantage, boosting self-confidence, having a "go to" statement prepared, focusing on what you can achieve, and adopting an attitude that's conducive to success.

And, this last paragraph I am going to discuss in detail later on.

When under pressure, people may tend to overthink the situation, or react with overconfidence. Not really the expected flight or fight answer. And, each type of behavior has undesirable results. To avoid overthinking situations, you should try to stay focused on what you're doing and just do what you do. You also need to remember to strive for progress and not perfection, and try to set a time limit for what needs to be done. Try to break tasks into smaller ones that are more manageable.

To resist the potentially damaging consequences of overconfidence, stay humble and accountable. Remember that good decision-making requires that you understand your limits and responsibilities. Make an effort to learn from your previous mistakes and stay realistic about the time and effort a task will take. It's one obvious tool to help us stay away from pressure. Get into the habit of thinking ahead about what may go wrong, and plan for these possibilities.

Stressful situations tend to distort how a situation is perceived. And, you need discipline to see the real picture. Discipline and one simple **four steps strategy that you can follow to optimize your perception of situations**.

First, notice and understand your automatic thoughts. These thoughts often arise from emotional reactions to situations and may go undetected at first. Second, identify thought distortions. Common types of thought distortions include having a negative bias, blame, emotive reasoning, and exaggeration.

The third step is to question whether there is any evidence for this kind of thinking. The fourth step is to revise your thoughts. This involves restating them in a more positive way, by separating them from any emotional or automatic thinking. And, I do agree, it sounds difficult the first time. But, with time this will become just another good behavior that you exhibit.

There's also a **four-step method you can follow for taking action in high-pressure situations**. First, you question the challenge. This involves asking how urgent the challenge is, how much time you have to address it, and what, if any, additional information you need to be able to respond to it. It doesn't take that much, and the benefits of not reacting before thinking, heavily outweigh the time spent doing it.

The second step is to identify your goal. This can be accomplished by asking yourself what you need to achieve in that particular situation, and as specific as SMART as possible. The third step is to generate and evaluate possible solutions. Here you should imagine alternative solutions, think of any potential positive and negative effects they may have, discuss them with a colleague or mentor, and finally select the most acceptable one.

The fourth step is to design a plan of action. Begin by dividing what needs to be done into manageable tasks, and assign specific times for accomplishing each. Finally, make sure that one element can be done immediately to build momentum toward your goal. You are the only one responsible with keeping you motivated under pressure. Others might help, but what you do is decisive.

So, to conclude this short part of our intro, performing under pressure can be difficult if we don't have the skills to make it easy. It's common for people to respond by overthinking or with overconfidence, both of which can lead people to perform below their abilities. To avoid these tendencies, you should aim to optimize your perceptions by recognizing distortions and revising negative thoughts. And, finally, it's helpful to rely on a process for taking action in high-pressure situations.

I read the sort of books that I am writing now to learn something, and I revisit if needed. And, most of the time I read for work, I read to use the experience of other people and to expand my understanding of specific issues. And, for this reason I added to this book a work relationships dimension. It matters under pressure and this is one useful skill to master.

Good working relationships are characterized by trust, openness, interrelatedness, respect, and effective communication. And pressure, obviously, can cause individuals to react negatively, and compromise good working relationships. Pressure can reduce awareness of others, sensitivity to others, communication, and collaboration. These effects can be made more extreme depending on the work styles of the individuals under pressure.

The four work styles are expressives, drivers, amiables, and analysts. Under pressure, expressives can go on the offensive, drivers can become dictatorial, amiables may become acquiescent, and analysts may become excessively detached from others. There are circumstances in the workplace where interactions with colleagues can generate pressure. Reacting negatively to colleagues in pressure situations can be damaging to work relationships.

And here also you will learn a **four-step technique that can help you handle stressful interactions**. First, monitor your feelings and tendencies toward instinctive or automatic responses. Then use a diversion to avoid being dominated by negative thoughts. Next, replace negative and distorted thoughts with positive thoughts. Finally, prepare to interact positively.

CHAPTER TWO

*Developing the Right Attitude for Performing
under Pressure*

Defining Pressure

It's almost certain that you'll have to deal with high pressure situations during your career and your life. Needless to say. Some professionals, such as airline pilots or firefighters, deal with very high levels of pressure on a daily basis. And, regardless of the scale of pressure — whether you're trying to land a plane suffering engine failure or trying to meet a production target — it's important that you manage the pressure effectively.

Pressure can be defined in different ways. It can be a compelling or constraining influence that affects your thought processes or willpower. For example, moral force can be used to bring pressure to bear on an individual. Pressure can manifest itself as an urgent claim or demand that can arise in business situations. Targets and deadlines can create pressure. And, a person may feel pressurized to perform.

Another definition of pressure is the state of physical, mental, social, or economic distress that can arise in stressful situations. The feeling of being under pressure is often linked to an individual's desire to be or to do something more. A new employee may feel the pressure of wanting to make it onto the management program or a person may want to exercise more as part of a healthy lifestyle. The need that drives both these examples can create pressure.

Causes of Pressure

If you stop for a second and think of some situations where you experienced pressure, and list the factors that caused you to feel pressure, you will realize that one of the factors you may have mentioned and that can cause pressure is the fear of embarrassment associated with failure. For example, if you have to perform an unfamiliar task, you may begin to doubt yourself. The possibility of failing to complete the task creates pressure for you.

The pressure that you may experience from a fear of failure has two sources: internal and external. The internal source is the anxiety that you generate inside yourself, and the external source is the unfamiliar task or environment that you face.

An Individual Experience

Pressure is a very individual experience. What causes pressure differs from person to person. Take Linda and Ned for example. Both work in the Finance Department of a large pharmaceutical company. Linda feels under pressure when she has to make presentations. Ned, on the other hand, is comfortable making presentations but feels pressure when he's asked to generate expense forecasts.

Exercise - What is Pressure?

Now, taking into account what you have learned, I hope that you are ready for a question. Of course, you can just skip this exercise if this is too easy. But, just in case, which of the following statements about pressure are accurate?

1 - Pressure can be a compelling or constraining influence.

2 - Pressure can arise because of an urgent claim or demand

3 - Pressure is associated with a desire to achieve more or to do more 4. Fear of failure can cause pressure

5 - Only external sources cause pressure

6 - Pressure is a uniform experience for everyone

And, the point is not to make this difficult, as you will see during this book, but to help you referring to fresh information with the aim of moving it into the long term memory for later use.

And — to compare — here are the potential answers with some contextual explanations:

Option 1: This option is correct. Pressure can cause a person to act, or prevent a person from acting. Option 2: This option is also correct. This is especially true in a business environment where deadlines and targets are common.

Option 3: This option is again correct. Wanting to have higher levels of achievement and desiring to do more with your life, professionally and personally, are motivating factors that can cause pressure.

Option 4: This option is also correct. Pressure is linked with the fear of failure or embarrassment. For example, a new employee is asked to perform a basic task but begins to experience pressure because of the fear of failure.

Option 5: This option is incorrect. There are both internal and external sources that can cause pressure. An example of an internal source of pressure is the potential angst you create for yourself when faced with a difficult task.

Option 6: This option is incorrect. Pressure is not a uniform experience for everyone. For example, some people experience pressure due to performance anxiety, whereas others feel pressure when faced with complex tasks.

What is Pressure?

So, the correct answers here are the following:

1. Pressure can be a compelling or constraining influence.

2. Pressure can arise because of an urgent claim or demand.

3. Pressure is associated with a desire to achieve more or to do more. And,

4. Fear of failure can cause pressure.

Managing Pressure

Often, people say that they perform well under pressure. Or, that they can't reach optimum performance without some element of pressure. And, yes, I have to admit that it's true. I said it before, pressure can be both energizing and invigorating. However, pressure can have a seriously negative impact when it isn't properly managed.

Poorly managed pressure in the workplace leads to excessive stress. This can be triggered by high profile events and situations. But it can also arise from the relentless daily grind of dealing with minor issues. When someone experiences too much pressure, too often and without a chance to recover, this lead to negative stress. Just as pressure is felt differently by individuals, so is work-related stress. How a person experiences stress depends on the person's personality and how that person manages pressure.

For example, Carl is the owner of an IT company. He enjoys handling important duties such as meeting new customers and finalizing product designs. But he finds that he experiences stress when he has to deal with dozens of minor administration requests on an everyday basis.

Stress-Related Outcomes

Stress can lead to negative emotions such as anger, anxiety, and depression. These emotions result in stress-related outcomes that can disrupt a person's ability to perform at work.

- The first outcome is that the person loses focus.
- The second is the person is unable to make decisions.
- And, the third is that the person is unable to perform under pressure.

Losing focus

Stress can lead to a person losing focus because the pressure the person was experiencing has ceased to be energizing or invigorating. The positive energies have been replaced by negative thoughts that preoccupy or distract a person from the task at hand.

For instance, Tom is an IT project manager. He loses focus during a project to replace a company's outdated operating system. He copes well initially and uses the pressure to drive his performance. But a series of setbacks on the project turns the pressure into negative stress. Tom becomes agitated and irritable. He's distracted because the situation is stressful and forgets to place an important software order. This causes delays in the project and increases his level of stress.

Decision-Making Impairment

Stress affects a person's ability to make the right decisions. To make a decision, a person uses cognitive and emotional intelligences. Stress greatly reduces a person's ability to use these capacities, with the result that the wrong decision is often made.

For example, Corinne is a marketing executive with a bank. She's working on a promotional strategy for a new financial product. Her stress levels are very high. She decides that the strategy should target young people in the 18 to 30 year old category. However, the product is more suitable for people in an older age group with their own homes. Corinne's manager is unhappy with her mistake. Corinne made the wrong decision because stress prevented her from using the right blend of cognitive and emotional intelligence.

Inability to perform under pressure

When people experience stress it's likely that any additional pressure they may feel will become negative and turn to stress also. This can lead to a paralyzing circle for those who are stressed. They inadvertently use their energies to undermine their own abilities because they feel overwhelmed. Instead of looking for positives, they can only see the negative side of their situation.

Consider Marsha, for example. She's a customer service operator for a chain of hotels. She's experiencing stress because guests' credit cards have incorrectly been charged twice. She has to arrange for the money to be refunded to each card and call each guest to apologize and explain why the error happened. She finds it difficult to cope with this task. When her manager asks her to draft the latest promotional e-mail outlining special offers she convinces herself that she can't cope, even though this is a task she has done many times before.

Pressurized Work Situations

A pressurized work situation can quickly become stressful because of uncertainty. When you have control over an event and there's a high level of predictability regarding its outcome, you are more relaxed about it. This is because a controlled and predictable event or task can be prepared for. However, when an unpredictable event occurs, you may begin to feel pressure. Having to operate outside your comfort zone and deal with unfamiliar factors increases the chances of stress.

This type of stress is anxiety-related. Doubts may begin to undermine your confidence. Questions such as "Will I get this done?" or "Will it be right?" raise levels of self-doubt and turn pressure into excessive stress.

Take Serge, for instance. He's a business strategy consultant. A client asks him to prepare a report on conducting business in the European Union. Serge usually works well under pressure, but he has very little experience in advising clients about this area. He feels pressure because the situation is new to him. And he experiences anxiety-related stress because he can't control or predict what happens next.

Exercise - When Pressure Becomes Stress

So, after all this theory what do you think? Which statements about the relationship between pressure and stress are accurate?

1 - Pressure can cause excessive stress.

2 - Stress can lead to a person experiencing negative emotions.

3 - Uncertainty can cause pressure to become stressful

4 - Only high profile events and major situations can lead to stress

5. Personality doesn't affect how a person experiences stress

Not a complicate exercise, and an obvious trick to play with new information to make it stick.

Option 1: This option is correct. When pressure isn't properly managed, stress can become a problem.

Option 2: This option is correct. Stress can cause a person to feel angry, anxious, and depressed.

Option 3: This option is correct. When faced with an uncertain situation or set of events, a person who is under pressure is more likely to experience stress.

Option 4: This option is incorrect. Stress can be caused by minor everyday occurrences, as well as high profile events and major situations.

Option 5: This option is incorrect. Personality as well as a person's ability to manage pressure does affect how stress is experienced. For example, a person who is very demanding and temperamental is likely to experience pressure if things begin to go wrong.

The Relationship Between Pressure and Stress

So, the correct answers here are the following:

1 - Pressure can cause excessive stress.

2 - Stress can lead to a person experiencing negative emotions

3-Uncertainty can cause pressure to become stressful

Pressure Triggers

Everyone reacts differently to pressure. And everyone's pressure trigger is different. There are four work-related factors that can trigger pressure: time pressure, work overload, relationship strain, and a necessity of balancing competing interests. Feeling under time pressure is usually a result of tight deadlines imposed by demanding schedules, and feeling underprepared for tasks.

The pressure to meet deadlines can be very intense. This is particularly true in situations where other people or functions are depending on the work being completed on time. If a person is given an important task, pressure may be triggered by the feeling of not being prepared because there isn't enough time.

Amber, for example, is an editorial assistant with a publishing company. She has been asked to proofread a new book before it is sent to the Design Department and the Printing Department. Amber feels pressure because she has a tight deadline and because of the difficulty of the task. She feels that she doesn't have enough time to prepare and won't be able to complete the task on time. She doesn't want to cause delays for the other departments.

Work Overload

Work overload is the second main trigger of job pressure. A person faced with a lot of work to do will naturally feel under some pressure. There are two different kinds of work overload: quantitative and qualitative.

Quantitative

A quantitative workload occurs when there's a large quantity of work to do. Consider an example of quantitative work overload leading to pressure. Jane works for a company that provides construction materials. At the end of the month, she has to process the invoices for every order. Because there are hundreds of invoices, Jane feels under severe pressure.

Qualitative

A qualitative workload involves work that requires close attention to detail and is time consuming. It differs from a quantitative workload because the emphasis isn't on the scale of the work. The quality of the work is what's important. For example, Kelly is a laboratory technician. Her job is to run a series of tests on samples of drinking water from local reservoirs to determine their purity. This task is very time consuming and intricate. And there's no margin for error. Kelly experiences pressure because of this qualitative work overload.

Relationship Pressure

The third triggering factor is relationship pressure. Working relationships are very important but can be complicated.

Dealing with difficult colleagues can lead to pressure because a person's role in the workplace can be undermined and made harder if a colleague is hostile, uncommunicative, or uncooperative. The desire to please is another aspect of relationship pressure. A person may feel shy or insecure and want to be accepted in the workplace. In addition to the person's working duties, this desire to please brings added pressure.

Consider this example. Frank is a junior architect who has just finished college. He has been hired by a firm, but finds his new colleagues very distant and unhelpful. Because this is his first job as a qualified architect, he's eager to please. However, he's finding it hard to deal with his colleagues. Frank experiences pressure because his colleagues are difficult to deal with and because he wants to please them and be accepted by them.

Balancing Competing Interests

The necessity of balancing competing interests is the fourth factor that can trigger pressure. This could involve a conflicting work role such as wanting to satisfy an employer and a customer.

For example, Tina, a computer hardware salesperson, feels pressure when she has to take on a conflicting work role. One of Tina's biggest customers places an order for a number of desktop computers. The customer has bought the same product before and was satisfied. Tina's manager urges her to try to sell a newer and more expensive version of the product to the customer. Tina is uncomfortable in this situation. But she wants to please her manager and her customer. This situation causes her to experience pressure.

Exercise II - Factors That Trigger Pressure

And, now is time for a couple of exercises.

Maria is an office manager with a credit ratings company. She needs to address a communication issue that has occurred between herself and Molly, the payroll administrator. She receives an e-mail from head office asking that she secure a cheaper rate from the office's long-term stationery supplier. What factors that could trigger pressure does Maria face?

1 - Relationship strain.

2 - Balancing competing interests.

3 - Time pressure.

4 - Recruitment concerns.

The right answers are presented bellow:

Option 1: This option is correct. Handling the communication issue she has with Molly could trigger pressure for Maria.

Option 2: This option is correct. Trying to secure a cheaper rate could create a work conflict for Maria, if she wants to please her employer and the supplier.

Option 3: This option is incorrect. In this scenario, Maria doesn't face any time pressure.

Option 4: This option is incorrect. Maria doesn't experience any recruitment concerns that could trigger pressure in this scenario.

Situations That Trigger Pressure (see case presented above)

1 - Relationship strain.

2 - Balancing competing interests.

Exercise II - Factors That Trigger Pressure

Zack is the supervisor of a retail store. His manager has asked him to finish taking inventory by the end of the week. He also has to write the vacation schedule for the store's 120 employees. What factors that could trigger pressure does Zack face?

1 - Time pressure.

2 - Work overload.

3 - Legislative requirements

4 - Health and safety

The right answers are presented bellow:

Option 1: This option is correct. Zack faces a deadline to complete the inventory count.

Option 2: This option is correct. Writing the holiday schedule for 120 employees could cause Zack to feel pressure.

Option 3: This option is incorrect. In this scenario, Zack doesn't have to deal with any legislative requirements.

Option 4: This option is incorrect. Health and safety isn't a concern in this scenario.

Situations That Trigger Pressure (see case presented above)

1 - Time pressure.

2 - Work overload.

To Conclude

Pressure can be energizing or invigorating, but without proper management it can cause excessive stress. Too much stress can lead to diminished focus, impaired judgment, and reduced ability to perform under pressure. Causes of pressure vary between individuals but there are four factors that are common causes of pressure in the workplace. These are time pressure, work overload, relationship strain, and having to balance competing interests.

You and How Stress Affects You

Pressure can cause you to react in different ways. Sometimes pressure can be an invigorating force that helps you achieve excellent results. But, on the other hand, pressure can be debilitating and hinder your ability to perform. It can be an opportunity for you to thrive, or a threat because it may lead to excessive stress.

To effectively manage your stress, you have to get a better understanding of how you respond to it. There are essentially two aspects to this. First, you need to consider who you are — that is, what characteristics you have that may make you more prone to excessive stress. And second, you need to consider how stress affects you in many different ways.

Responding to Stress

Your response to a stressful situation you experience depends in part on who you are. Who you are is determined by your attitudes, beliefs, and values; your past experience; your personality; and your preferences.

So, in what way do think your attitudes, beliefs, and values affect how you experience pressure?

You may think that your attitudes, beliefs, and values affect how you respond to stress because they relate to how you think and feel about pressure. You might have a very positive attitude toward pressure and use it to boost your performance. Or you might view pressure in a negative way and allow it to turn into stress, which can limit your potential.

Beliefs and Values

Your beliefs and values represent what you stand for and what's right and wrong for you. They can cause you to respond negatively to pressure when you're faced with a situation where you're unable to honor them. Or they can give you the inner strength to calmly perform duties that might otherwise create a heavy burden of stress.

For example, Alex is a warehouse supervisor. He usually has a positive attitude toward pressure. He welcomes and uses pressure to push his performance levels at work. But Alex's beliefs and values affect how he responds to the pressure of implementing his company's waste disposal policies. He is a dedicated environmentalist, and he believes that his company doesn't take its recycling responsibilities seriously. He becomes stressed because the waste policies don't feel right to him.

Past Experiences

Your past experiences of dealing with situations that cause pressure and stress will affect how you deal with current and future situations. Whether the past experiences were positive or negative, they'll have had a formative effect on you. How these situations turned out in the past influences how you will feel about upcoming situations.

If you dealt with a stressful situation successfully on a prior occasion, you'll probably be confident dealing with future situation of the same kind. But if your handling of the similar situation in the past went badly, this will make you feel much more uncertain about dealing with the current situation.

Take Grace, for instance. She works in a customer service call center. Last year, when some of her colleagues were on their annual summer vacations, the number of calls Grace had to answer increased. She didn't respond positively to this pressure and the situation became very stressful for her. She's not looking forward to the same situation when some of her colleagues will be away this summer.

Personality

Another part of considering who you are is to analyze your own personality. Some aspects of the personality you developed in your early years may remain with you for the rest of your life.

This doesn't mean that you can't learn to think differently or change your behavior. But it does mean that you're likely to respond in a certain way when faced with particular types of situations. High-pressure situations can bring a person's personality traits to the forefront.

Exercise - Responding to Stress

What statements about how who you are affects the way you respond to stress are true?

1 - Your values don't influence how you react to stress in the workplace.

2 - Past experiences can determine how you approach a stressful situation.

3 - Some of your personality traits have a bearing on how you respond to stress-related situations.

4 - Attitude doesn't affect how a person responds to stress.

Bellow are the answers discussed briefly:

Option 1: This option is incorrect. Values do influence how a person responds to stress. Values represent what's right and wrong for a particular individual. Normal pressure will be intensified if the situation contravenes a person's system of values.

Option 2: This option is correct. Your past experiences can determine whether or not you will approach a stressful situation in a positive or negative way.

Option 3: This option is correct. Aspects of your personality can influence how you handle stressful situations.

Option 4: This option is incorrect. Attitude can affect your response to stress. If, for example, you enjoy your work, you are less likely to be excessively stressed by the pressures associated with it.

Responding to Stress

2 - Past experiences can determine how you approach a stressful situation

3 - Some of your personality traits have a bearing on how you respond to stress-related situations

Anxiety

The first important aspect of personality in relation to stress is anxiety-proneness. If making small and insignificant decisions causes you to become anxious, this means that you're highly prone to anxiety. If you only become anxious when faced with very daunting decisions or situations, you're less prone to anxiety. For example, Dawn is an air traffic controller. Although she makes crucial decisions every day, she very rarely becomes anxious under pressure.

Optimism

Another aspect of your personality to consider is your general outlook. Whether you're generally an optimistic or pessimistic person will have a bearing on your response to stress. Unsurprisingly, those who have a more optimistic disposition are better able to cope with stressful situations than those who tend to be pessimistic. If you expect the worst outcome from a situation, it's clearly more difficult to cope with it.

Consider this example. Julio owns his own printing company. He has an optimistic outlook. His company receives an order to print a retail supplier's product catalog. But one of Julio's main printers breaks down. He is in danger of missing the deadline. Faced with this pressure, he decides to outsource some of the printing to another firm. He finishes the order on time. His optimism prevented him from buckling under the pressure.

Perfectionism

Perfectionism is another personality trait that can influence your response to stress in a major way. Perfectionists want to get every detail right, and this desire to have everything perfect brings its own pressures. A perfectionist is more likely to experience stress than someone who doesn't always hold everything to such high standards. Perfectionists can get frustrated over tiny mistakes; they overwork trying to get everything just right, but sometimes nothing ever completely pleases them.

For example, Dean is an interior designer, redesigning the interior of an old hotel. He is a perfectionist and demands that every detail be carried out as he has specified. Due to the massive scale of the project and his exacting requirements, Dean begins to feel enormous pressure that quickly turns to negative stress.

Attitudes and Values

And finally, in addition to considering your attitudes and values, your past experiences, and your personality, you should also consider your own preferences. These preferences become second nature and can affect how you respond to stress.

For example, you may have a preference for taking risks rather than using tried and tested methods. Or you may prefer to work with detail rather than rely on speculative ideas. The risk-taking preference is likely to involve more pressure and stress than the working with detail preference.

Kate, for instance, is a laboratory technician. She has a preference for making her decisions based on sound logic rather than intuition or a gut feeling. This methodical approach reduces the level of stress that she faces because she doesn't allow unknown elements to influence her decisions.

Exercise I - Personality Traits and Stress

Match the examples to the aspect of a person's personality that influences them.

Options:

A - A construction worker experiences stress completing relatively minor tasks.

B - A stockbroker's relentlessly negative attitude contributes to her high stress levels

C - An electrician's determination to micromanage every part of a task adds to his stress levels

Targets:

1 - Anxiety-proneness.

2 - General outlook.

3 - Perfectionism.

Personality Traits and Stress

When minor tasks cause an individual to feel stress, this person is someone with an anxiety-prone personality.

When stress arises because of a negative attitude, it means the person is an individual with a pessimistic general outlook.

Feeling stress because of a desire to micromanage tasks means the person is a perfectionist. Correct answer(s):

Target 1 = Option A

Target 2 = Option B

Target 3 = Option C

Exercise II - Personality Traits and Stress

Verne is a software salesperson. He has been reassigned by his manager to focus on selling payroll software to customers in the retail sector. He is unhappy with this switch as he was happier selling data management software to customers in the government sector. He previously sold products to customers in the retail sector and he found it to be very demanding and time consuming.

He believes that the switch will increase the pressure associated with his job and make it even more difficult to make sales. The fact that he has to familiarize himself with a new product and develop a new sales pitch causes him to worry, even though he doesn't favor a particular sales style, nor is he concerned about how he makes the sale.

What characteristics does Verne have that might make him prone to stress?

Options:

1 - Attitudes, beliefs, values, confidence
2 - Past experience
3 - Anxiety proneness
4 - Preferences
5 - Perfectionism

Answer:

Option 1: This option is correct. Verne has a negative attitude toward the sector he has been asked to sell to.

Option 2: This option is correct. Verne's previous experience of selling to the retail sector wasn't good. Option 3: This option is correct. Verne becomes anxious because he has to familiarize himself with a new product and develop a new sales pitch.

Option 4: This option is incorrect. Verne has no preferences in relation to how he sells. Option 5: This option is incorrect. Verne isn't concerned about how he makes a sale.

Personality Traits and Stress

1 - Attitudes, beliefs, values, confidence.
2 - Past experience.
3 - Anxiety proneness.

Use this job aid to review the factors to consider in relation to your response to stress

Factors to consider in relation to your response to stress

Consider who you are	Consider whether you choose to get stressed	Consider how stress affects
Your attitudes, beliefs, values, and confidence	Sources of pressure	Physically
Your past experience	Patterns of thinking	Cognitively
Your personality		Emotionally
Anxiety-proneness		Behaviorally
General outlook		
Perfectionism		
Preferences		

Ways in Which Stress Affects You

To complete your understanding of your response to stress, you should be aware of the different ways stress affects you. Stress can manifest itself in physical, cognitive, emotional, or behavioral ways. These symptoms may have other origins than stress, but they are potential indicators of stress that should be considered nonetheless.

There are four physical symptoms that have been associated with stress: sleeping fitfully, agitated behavior, muscle tension, and lack of energy. And among the cognitive symptoms of stress are mental slowness, confusion, constant worry, and difficulty concentrating.

When it comes to the emotional side of stress, these four symptoms are typical: irritation, no sense of humor, frustration, and apathy. Behavioral symptoms of stress include poor work relations, a sense of loneliness, avoiding others, and not taking time to relax.

Exercise - Symptoms of Stress

Match the symptoms of stress to the appropriate categories. Each category may have more than one match.

Options:

A - A sales manager loses sleep thinking about targets.

B - A journalist working on a deadline shows signs of annoyance.

C - An accountant consults an online guide to remember a simple tax rate.

D - A stressed office administrator feels a sense of loneliness.

E - A web site designer feels frustrated because of a heavy workload

F - Stress causes a nurse to constantly worry

Targets:

1 - Physical.

2 - Cognitive.

3 - Emotional.

4 - Behavioral.

Answer:

Losing sleep is an example of one of the physical symptoms associated with stress. Other symptoms include agitated behavior, muscle tension, and lack of energy.

Forgetting simple things because of mental slowness, and constant worrying are both cognitive symptoms of stress. Other symptoms include confusion and difficulty concentrating.

Becoming irritated because of deadline-related stress and feeling frustrated due to a mounting workload are emotional symptoms of stress. Other emotional symptoms include apathy and having no sense of humor.

Feeling a sense of loneliness because of stress is a behavioral symptom of stress. Other such symptoms are poor work relations, avoiding others, and not taking time to relax.

Correct answer(s):

Target 1 = Option A

Target 2 = Option C, Option F

Target 3 = Option B, Option E

Target 4 = Option D

Restoring the Balance

Experiencing excessive stress triggers different emotions in a person that cause an imbalance to occur. Instead of being calm, a person becomes worried or begins to act in an uncharacteristic manner. To restore the balance and neutralize the impact of stress, the human body releases endorphins.

This can have serious consequences because endorphins dull a person's ability to think and feel. Both abilities affect a person's decision-making and interpersonal skills. This is why stress can impair your work performance.

If you want to perform to the best of your ability at work, you need to successfully manage your relationships, imagination, emotions, and cognition. Stress that is caused by pressure can negatively affect these areas.

Impact of Stress

The following areas are negatively impacted by stress:

- Relationships

- Imagination
- Emotions
- Cognition

Relationships

Stress can negatively affect your working relationships by making you less sensitive to the needs of others and by reducing your ability to show empathy.

To survive a stressful situation, you might block out other people and concentrate on doing everything you can to relieve the stress. This survival mechanism reduces your interpersonal skills and can lead to workplace conflict.

For example, Violet is a teller in a bank. She is experiencing stress because her computer system keeps crashing and there's a long line of customers waiting. Her colleague Penny — who has just started working for the bank — asks her a question about a currency exchange rate but Violet dismisses her with a shrug. Penny's feelings are hurt.

Imagination

High stress can have a negative impact on your imagination by diminishing your ability to think in a creative way. That's because it puts a physiological and psychological strain on the human brain, which compromises creativity.

This can have serious implications in the workplace because imagination is a key driver of business innovation.

Take Leroy, an advertising executive. He's feeling stressed because he has been asked to create a new advertising concept for a client. Because the stress affects Leroy's creativity, he struggles to come up with any ideas. Instead he reuses a concept that he developed three years ago for a different client. His current client is unhappy with his efforts.

Emotions

Stress can also affect your emotions in unhelpful ways. It can cause your enthusiasm, interest, and motivation to wane. It can also increase your moodiness and irritability. And it can give you a feeling of being increasingly overwhelmed, which can cause you to disconnect from your work.

Take Myra, for instance. She's an IT project manager and is responsible for rolling out a new operating system for a large multinational corporation. The project starts well and Myra is looking forward to the challenge but the scale of it quickly causes her to feel under pressure. She experiences stress and this leads her to lose her earlier enthusiasm for the project. Now, she feels as if she can't wait for it to end.

As her stress levels increase, the members of her team notice that she's prone to erratic mood swings and seems irritated when approached. When the project reaches its halfway point, Myra begins to feel completely overwhelmed and, as a result, tries to distance herself from the project.

Exercise I - Performance and Pressure-Induced Stress

Grant is the lead designer for a car manufacturing company. He and his team have been asked to design a prototype for a new child seat. Grant begins to experience stress. He assigns tasks to each member of the team. He insists that the initial design should be completed using computer aided design software.

A team member has a personal issue that she needs to take care of. Grant refuses to listen and instructs her to go back to work. Grant can't think of any design ideas for the child seat so he browses competitors' web sites for ideas. At a meeting to review progress, Grant is very curt. Soon after, his team notices that he seems reluctant to engage in the project. He stops asking his team for daily updates.

In what ways did Greg demonstrate impaired performance due to pressure-induced stress?

Options:

1 - He delegated tasks to other team members.

2 - He insists on using computer aided design software.

3 - He refused to listen to his colleague who had a personal issue.

4 - He browses competitors' web sites for ideas.

5 - He is curt in the progress meeting.

6 - He stops asking for daily updates.

7 - He's reluctant to engage in the project.

Answer:

Option 1: This option is incorrect. Delegating tasks is a fundamental role for any team leader.

Option 2: This option is incorrect. Using computer aided design is quicker and more accurate than relying on manual processes.

Option 3: This option is correct. Greg's refusal to listen to his colleague showed that his sensitivity and empathy were affected by stress.

Option 4: This option is correct. Greg's imagination and creativity were hindered by stress to such an extent that he couldn't generate his own ideas.

Option 5: This option is correct. Greg's moody reaction in the progress meeting indicates that his emotions were affected by stress.

Option 6: This option is correct. By no longer asking for daily updates, Grant demonstrates that stress has caused his enthusiasm for the project to wane.

Option 7: This option is correct. Grant's reluctance to engage in the project indicates that stress has caused him to feel overwhelmed.

Correct answer(s):

3 - He refused to listen to his colleague who had a personal issue.

4 - He browses competitors' web sites for ideas.

5 - He is curt in the progress meeting.

6 - He stops asking for daily updates.

7 - He's reluctant to engage in the project.

- **Cognition**

Stress can disrupt your cognitive functions by inhibiting your ability to concentrate and focus. It can also cause memory lapses and impair your decision making. Stress can have a disruptive influence on your thought processes by causing you to view everything in a negative way.

For example, Krista is a claims assessor with an insurance company. She has a large case load to work through and her manager has set a deadline for completing the assessment of each claim. This creates a stressful situation for her. As the deadline approaches, she finds that she isn't able to focus on the details of each claim. She also forgets to double-check the information provided in the claims.

The pressure impairs her good judgment and she decides to recommend that all the claims are valid. From her previous experience, she knows that this very rarely happens — there are always some dubious claims. But she still goes ahead with the decision. She begins to regret her decision to work in the insurance industry.

Exercise II - Performance and Pressure-Induced Stress

The examples represent actions of people who are under pressure, but which examples illustrate impaired performance due to pressure-induced stress?

Options:

1 - An electrician is easily distracted from the rewiring job he's supposed to be doing.

2 - A retail manager forgets the combination to the store's safe.

3 - A secretary opens an e-mail even though her anti-virus software warns her not to.

4 - A security consultant can't find any positives in his career

5. A mechanic decides that it's too risky not to fix the brakes

6. An airline pilot decides that the weather conditions are unsuitable for take-off

Answer:

Option 1: This option is correct. Stress can prevent a person from focusing on a task.

Option 2: This option is correct. Stress can cause individuals to suffer memory lapses.

Option 3: This option is correct. Stress can impair a person's decision-making abilities.

Option 4: This option is correct. Stress can cause a person to be excessively negative.

Option 5: This option is incorrect. Not taking a risk with safety represents good decision-making under pressure.

Option 6: This option is incorrect. Choosing not to fly during bad weather shows good judgment under pressure.

Correct answer(s):

1 - An electrician is easily distracted from the rewiring job he's supposed to be doing 2. A retail manager forgets the combination to the store's safe.

3 - A secretary opens an e-mail even though her anti-virus software warns her not to 4. A security consultant can't find any positives in his career.

To Conclude

Pressure can be a positive force that helps you achieve excellent results. But, on the other hand, pressure can be debilitating and hinder your ability to perform when it causes excessive stress.

To understand your response to stress, you need to consider who you are — your attitudes and values, your personality, your past experiences, and your preferences. And you also need to learn to recognize potential symptoms of stress — physical, emotional, cognitive, and behavioral.

It's also important to realize the different ways that stress can impair your work performance by negatively impacting on your creativity, decision-making, emotions, and interpersonal skills.

Use this follow-on activity to review your response to pressure. Consider these questions to analyze your response to pressure.

1 - What type of pressure do you experience most?

2 - What aspects of your personality predispose you to react in certain ways?

3 - What is your attitude to pressure?

4 - What symptoms of stress do you most encounter?

Work-related pressure can occur in any profession or industry. In some situations, it can lead to stress and this can cause suboptimal performance. Maybe you know a colleague who is very competent and efficient. But in pressurized situations, that person's ability and judgment becomes seriously impaired.

This is why it's crucial to develop the right attitude while under pressure. Doing so will help you to optimize your performance, increase your energy levels, recognize opportunities, and respond creatively to challenges.

Benefits of the Right Attitude

The first benefit of developing the right attitude while under pressure is that it can optimize your performance. An optimistic and positive outlook will help you to achieve your goals.

Strengthen Your Resilience

Optimism can strengthen your resilience. In difficult situations when you're experiencing pressure, you need to stand firm. Having a positive attitude can make this easier to do.

Spence, for example, has recently qualified as an insurance actuary. He has an enthusiastic and positive attitude. This contributes to his levels of happiness and perseverance. Both these elements contribute to better levels of performance.

Increase Your Energy

The second benefit of developing the right attitude while under pressure is that it can increase your energy levels by controlling your stress. Stress can sap your energy and negatively affect your mood. If you don't control your stress, it may overwhelm you and reduce your productivity. Losing control over your stress causes you to focus your concentration on negative mental processes.

Because Spence is new to his position, he is experiencing stress. But he develops a positive approach to stress and uses his energy to concentrate on productive outcomes.

Recognizing Opportunities

Recognizing opportunities is the third benefit of cultivating the right attitude while under pressure. You should view pressure as an opportunity to find solutions.

The perceptions of people with negative attitudes tend to become skewed. If the boss makes a small criticism, it gets seen as an attack on your entire performance, which increases the feeling of pressure. But with the right attitude, you can find opportunities in what appear to be problems.

Spence maintains a positive attitude. Instead of being weighed down by the pressure of a tight deadline, he sees his assignment as an opportunity to show what he's capable of.

Respond Creatively to Challenges

The final benefit of developing the right attitude when under pressure is that it enables you to respond creatively to challenges. A positive attitude can free your mind to think creatively and laterally about a situation that is causing pressure. Spence for instance, uses many different perspectives such as entrepreneur, dreamer, optimist, strategist, and architect.

Exercise - Benefits of Having the Right Attitude

What are the benefits of having the right attitude while under pressure?

Options:

1 - Enhances performance.

2 - Raises energy levels.

3 - Allows you recognize opportunities.

4 - Helps you think creatively.

5 - Eliminates uncertainty.

6 - Guarantees success.

Answer:

Option 1: This option is correct. When you have a positive attitude, you are more likely to be able to achieve your goals.

Option 2: This option is correct. By developing the right attitude, you can raise your energy levels. You can achieve this by focusing on positive elements rather than dwelling on the negative aspects of your situation, which can be energy-sapping.

Option 3: This option is correct. By having the right attitude, you're less likely to adopt a negative perceptual bias. This means that you actively look for opportunities that you can develop.

Option 4: This option is correct. Adopting the right attitude under pressure allows you to find creative solutions.

Option 5: This option is incorrect. Eliminating uncertainty isn't one of the benefits of having the right attitude while under pressure.

Option 6: This option is incorrect. Having the right attitude can help you succeed, but it cannot guarantee success.

Correct Answer(s):

1 - Enhances performance.

2 - Raises energy levels.

3 - Allows you recognize opportunities.

4 - Helps you think creatively

Sometimes, despite your best efforts, you'll find that you can't control all the external factors that cause you to experience pressure. However, you can control your reaction to pressure. This will help you avoid wasting energy on negative emotions that can impede your performance at work. It's best to adopt an attitude of control for performing under pressure. Avoid making instinctive reactions. Think things through instead so that your reaction is more considered and appropriate.

Principles to Control Your Reaction

There are two main principles to follow to control your reaction to pressure. First, **take control of yourself**. And second, **cultivate a "success mentality."** But what does the first principle mean? Taking control of yourself means taking stock of your emotions, establishing a sense of calm, accepting that you can't control everything, and using self-talk as a reminder.

Taking stock of your emotions involves identifying what your feelings are when you're under pressure and how these feelings impact your behavior and your relationships with others. If you do this objectively, you'll create an early warning system for yourself.

For instance, if you're feeling frustrated because of pressure, will this make you difficult to approach? If you're able to anticipate the negative tendencies that these feelings cause, you may be able to avoid them.

Consider this example. Corbin is a quality control supervisor for a dairy processing company. In the past, pressure caused him to become withdrawn and his colleagues found it difficult to deal with him. After he identified this tendency in himself, Corbin made an effort to be more communicative if he felt under pressure. He found this actually relieved some of his stress.

Control Your Emotions

Another aspect of taking stock of your emotions is to realize that experiencing high pressure can cause you to lose control. As pressure increases, your responses may become more instinctive and reactive.

You should try to be more measured and precise in your responses when you're under pressure. Try not to let your emotions dictate how you respond.

Tina, for example, is a hospital administrator who was under pressure to quickly transfer a large number of patient details to a database. She grew irritable and responded harshly to a friendly query from a colleague. But when she realized the effect of her behavior, she became more aware of how she had lost control of her emotions. She is now determined to keep her reactions more controlled when she's under pressure.

Exercise - Manage Your Emotions

What examples demonstrate individuals taking stock of their emotions?

Options:

1 - A computer analyst recognizes that he is avoiding his colleagues because he's feeling under pressure.

2 - A bank manager learns to moderate her behavior while under pressure, so she doesn't lose control.

3 - An accountant uses his colleague's behavior under pressure as a model for how he should react.

4 - A health and safety inspector deals with pressure by putting pressure on members of his team.

Answer:

Option 1: This option is correct. Identifying how your feelings while under pressure can affect working relationships is an example of taking stock of your emotions. This process also involves how these feelings affect a person's behavior.

Option 2: This option is correct. Being aware that pressure can cause a person to lose control is an example of taking stock of your emotions.

Option 3: This option is incorrect. Using other people's emotions as a model for your own isn't an example of taking stock of your emotions.

Option 4: This option is incorrect. Transferring pressure onto others isn't an example of taking stock of your emotions.

Correct answer(s):

1. A computer analyst recognizes that he is avoiding his colleagues because he's feeling under pressure

2. A bank manager learns to moderate her behavior while under pressure, so she doesn't lose control

A Sense of Calm

49

Establishing a sense of calm is another aspect of taking control of yourself. When you begin to experience pressure, you need to make up your mind that you're going to stay calm.

A calm person is more likely to make the correct decision than a person who's nervous or overexcited. You should tell yourself that you're going to use the pressure to make yourself stronger and better. And to do this you need to remain calm.

For example, Liz is an architect who has been asked to project-manage the design of a new university campus. Because of the scale of the project, Liz begins to experience pressure. But she's determined to control her reactions. Every morning, before she goes to work, she looks in the mirror and tells herself that it's important to remain calm so that she can use the pressure to her advantage.

Accept What You Cannot Control

Accepting that you can't control everything is another helpful way of taking control of yourself. Remember, you can't always control the things that cause pressure, but you can control your reaction.

You should remind yourself that the difficulties that lead to pressure are a normal and unavoidable part of life. If you dwell on these difficulties or blow them out of proportion, you may experience various negative emotions that can make the situation worse.

Take Anita, for instance. She's the manager of a small catering company. Two members of her team become sick the day before the company is to provide catering for a conference. This situation puts enormous pressure on Anita. Instead of getting frustrated because of the circumstances, however, she decides to react positively to fulfill the catering contract.

Talk Yourself Into Calmness

Self-talk is a useful way to help you stay calm while under pressure. Self-talk should focus on positive thoughts and you should refuse to allow negative thoughts to dominate your mind. Also, don't dwell on past mistakes but concentrate on the issue at hand. There's nothing you can do about past mistakes now. Instead, use your energy to focus on the present.

For example, Rick is the owner of a medium-sized company that manufactures household appliances. It has recently been discovered that a large batch of one of the company's products has been shipped with an important part missing.

Rick has to recall the entire batch and apologize to customers. But instead of dwelling on this mistake and feeling negative, Rick takes positive action. He works with key members of his team to perfect the product assembly process.

He reminds himself that the pressure he's experiencing will pass and that the important thing is to see the problem as an opportunity to improve.

Exercise - Taking Control of Yourself

What examples represent actions that can help you take control of yourself in a pressurized situation?

Options:

1 - A computer games developer who is under pressure to complete a product becomes aware that he is being harsh with his colleague.

2 - A nurse facing a long shift reminds herself to remain calm so that she can make the right decisions.

3 - A realtor accepts that there'll always be pressure to make sales, but he can't control property prices.

4 - A marketing expert tells himself to concentrate on the present after a campaign to promote a product fails.

5 - A building contractor devotes his energy to discovering why the project has fallen behind schedule.

6 - A comic book store owner under pressure believes that it's impossible to compete with online retailers.

Answer:

Option 1: This option is correct. Taking stock of your emotions is an action that can help you to take control of yourself in a pressurized situation.

Option 2: This option is correct. Reminding yourself to remain calm is one of the actions that can help you to take control when faced with pressure.

Option 3: This option is correct. Accepting that you can't always control the causes of pressure is part of taking control of yourself in a pressurized situation.

Option 4: This option is correct. Reminding yourself to concentrate on the present is a way of using self-talk as a reminder to remain calm, which is one of the actions for taking control of yourself in a pressurized situation.

Option 5: This option is incorrect. Devoting your energy to a past problem rather than using positive energy to deal with the issue at hand isn't an example of an action for taking control of yourself in a pressurized situation.

Option 6: This option is incorrect. Allowing negative thoughts to dominate your mind isn't an example of an action for taking control of yourself in a pressurized situation.

Correct Answer(s):

1 - A computer games developer who is under pressure to complete a product becomes aware that he is being harsh with his colleague

2 - A nurse facing a long shift reminds herself to remain calm so that she can make the right decisions.

3 - A realtor accepts that there'll always be pressure to make sales, but he can't control property prices.

4 - A marketing expert tells himself to concentrate on the present after a campaign to promote a product fails.

The second principle when managing your attitude is to cultivate a "success mentality." This involves using your emotions to your advantage, boosting self-confidence, having a "go to" statement prepared, focusing on what you can achieve, and cultivating an attitude for success.

Using Your Emotions

Using your emotions to your advantage requires that you think of a past situation where you were under pressure. Recall the emotions that you felt and tell yourself that you no longer choose to be influenced negatively by these emotions. Instead, you're going to use them to your advantage and overcome this pressurized situation.

For example, Sidney is a TV producer. She experiences regular pressure because of deadlines. Each time she experiences pressure, she thinks back to her interview for the job. She felt extreme pressure then. Now she tells herself that those emotions won't affect her in this situation because she has grown stronger since then.

Boosting Self-Confidence

Boosting self-confidence is part of cultivating a "success mentality." It involves telling yourself that you'll make it through this high pressure situation. When you experience pressure, take some time to remove yourself from negative emotions. Then confirm to yourself that you will succeed.

Take Oliver, for instance. He's an executive with a telecommunications company. He has to negotiate with customers and finds this stressful. But he tells himself that he has what it takes to achieve success.

Preparing "Go To" Statements

Having a "go to" statement prepared is another way of cultivating a "success mentality." This type of statement can be used to build a positive self-image. The statement is something that you can repeat to yourself during pressurized situations to refocus your mind on to a positive path. A "go to" statement can be personally oriented or professionally oriented. Either type should remind you of your goals.

See bellow each type of "go to" statement for an example of it:

Personally oriented

"I will achieve my goals so that I can fulfill my potential."

Professionally oriented

"I am a highly skilled research scientist. I will help this company to be a success by conducting cutting-edge research and development"

Focus on Objective

Focusing on what you can achieve means that you should remove negative thoughts from your mind. But this is easier said than done when you are under pressure.

55

Negative thoughts can quickly take a foothold in your mind when you are under pressure. Thoughts such as, "I'm not able to do this" and "There's no use trying – it would be better to give up" can damage your confidence. To prevent these negative thoughts you need to counteract them with a thought-stopping statement like "Take control!" or "Don't go there."

For example, Jennifer is a client account manager with an advertising company. Sometimes when she's under pressure she gets negative thoughts that undermine her confidence in her own abilities. To stop these thoughts she says to herself, "Not now, not ever!"

Rise to the Challenge

Cultivating an attitude for success requires that your thoughts, feelings, and actions all display your willingness and desire to succeed, especially in high-pressure situations. Your overall demeanor has to demonstrate that you are prepared to rise to the challenge.

For instance, Nils is a maintenance engineer. He has a very heavy workload to get through. But he makes sure to stay positive by blocking negative thoughts. He convinces himself that he will be successful despite the pressure.

Exercise - Foster a "Success Mentality"

What examples demonstrate actions that can foster a "success mentality?"

Options:

1 - An insurance adjustor recalls how he felt in a previous pressurized situation.

2 - A trainee lawyer tells herself that she has the ability to succeed.

3 - An IT engineer repeats a statement to himself reminding him of his goals.

4 - An office administrator uses a thought-stopping statement to keep focused.

5 - A security officer concentrates on having a positive demeanor.

6 - An aircraft technician lists his negative thoughts.

7 - A pharmacist ignores any past experiences of pressure.

Answer:

Option 1: This option is correct. Recalling your feelings from a previous experience of pressure is an example of using your emotions to your advantage.

Option 2: This option is correct. Telling yourself that you have the ability to succeed is an example of boosting self-confidence.

Option 3: This option is correct. Having a "go to statement" prepared is an example of an action that can foster a "success mentality."

Option 4: This option is correct. Using a thought-stopping statement to remain focused is an example of focusing on what you can achieve.

Option 5: This option is correct. Concentrating on having a positive demeanor is an example of cultivating an attitude for success.

Option 6: This option is incorrect. Focusing on negative thoughts is not an action that can foster a "success mentality." It is better to focus on positive thoughts.

Option 7: This option is incorrect. Ignoring past experiences of pressure is not an action that can foster a "success mentality." Previous experiences can be used to provide impetus to succeed when faced with current pressurized situations.

Correct Answer(s):

1 - An insurance adjustor recalls how he felt in a previous pressurized situation.

2 - A trainee lawyer tells herself that she has the ability to succeed.

3 - An IT engineer repeats a statement to himself reminding him of his goals.

4 - An office administrator uses a thought-stopping statement to keep focused.

5 - A security officer concentrates on having a positive demeanor.

To Conclude

Developing the right attitude while under pressure can help you to optimize your performance, increase your energy levels, recognize opportunities, and respond creatively to challenges.

There are two main principles to help you control your reaction to pressure. First, you take control of yourself by taking stock of your emotions, establishing a sense of calm, accepting that you can't control everything, and using self-talk.

Second, you cultivate a "success mentality" by using your emotions to your advantage, boosting self-confidence, having a "go to" statement prepared, focusing on what you can achieve, and adopting an attitude that's conducive to success.

Taking control of yourself	Cultivating a "success mentality"
Take stock of your emotions	Use your emotions to your advantage
Establish a sense of calm	Boost self-confidence
Accept that you can't control everything	Have a "go to" statement prepared
Use self-talk as a reminder	Focus on what you can achieve
Use your emotions to your advantage Boost self-confidence	Cultivate an attitude for success
Have a "go to" statement prepared	
Focus on what you can achieve Cultivate an attitude for success	

CHAPTER THREE
Taking Action for Performing under Pressure

Overthinking and Overconfidence

Some people excel under pressure, while others struggle. In high-pressure situations, some people tend to adopt one of two kinds of behavior: overthinking or overconfidence. People who succeed when under pressure are often better at avoiding, or balancing, these tendencies.

To perform well under pressure you need to think sufficiently about what needs to be done, but not fall into the trap of overthinking your performance. Similarly, you should have confidence in your abilities and knowledge, but not to the point where your arrogance impairs your judgment.

Overthinking Under Pressure

Overthinking can lead to a sense of paralysis — of becoming so concerned about the details and outcomes of the situation that you don't know where to begin.

In high-pressure situations, some people tend to question their ability to perform. Others may try to control every variable. In either case, the focus is shifted away from what needs to be accomplished and toward the performance. This focus on performance can cause people to perform below their ability.

For example, Lenore works for an investment firm and has recently been granted control of her first account. Her first assignment in this new role is to do a risk analysis of an important client's portfolio.

Wanting to impress her boss, Lenore researches every conceivable variable of the client's portfolio. She's pleased to find a large volume of information, which she's sure will improve the accuracy of her report. Eventually, however, it begins to seem that each additional source she consults makes her less certain of her final analysis.

Finally, Lenore is surrounded by so much information that she becomes totally paralyzed and isn't able to finish the report on time.

Avoiding Overthinking

To avoid overthinking in high-pressure situations, you can use several strategies. First, stay focused on what you're trying to achieve. Second, try to just do what you do. Third, strive for progress instead of perfection. Fourth, set a time limit for your task and stick to it. And fifth, try to break the task down into smaller, simpler tasks.

Stay Focused

Staying focused on what you're trying to achieve, rather than on the details of your performance, is an effective way to avoid overthinking.

For example, Clarice needs to give a presentation. She's anxious because it will influence an important decision. Though she has given many presentations in the past, she can't help but worry that she might fail.

However, Clarice resists this type of thinking and instead focuses on her previous successes, which helps her to do the best job she can.

Just Do What You Do

Just doing what you do, rather than dwelling on what else you could or should do, can help you perform under pressure.

Consider Caesar, who is negotiating the sale of a property. He's performed well in several similar transactions in the past, but has started to doubt his negotiation strategy this time.

However, he knows that he has succeeded with this strategy in the past and can rely on it. By focusing on what he knows he can do, Caesar retains a sense of confidence and avoids self-doubt.

Seek Progress Not Perfection

When you're under pressure, try focusing your attention on making progress rather than achieving perfection.

When Angela started awarding contracts to bidding firms, she spent too long trying to find the perfect one.

Eventually, she realized that none of the firms were perfect and she made a decision after reviewing each proposal once.

Set a Time Limit

Setting a time limit on what you need to accomplish can help you to take action in pressured situations.

As a new architect, Andrew spent an incredible amount of overtime ensuring his first projects were perfect. While his commitment was appreciated, his superiors were concerned that he was exhausting himself.

They suggested he set time limits. Andrew now writes a schedule for each task in a project. This has helped him to keep moving on to the next task, which has increased his overall output without compromising his standards of excellence.

Break the Task Down

To avoid over-analysis, try breaking your task down into smaller, more manageable ones.

For example, Nina was reviewing a rights contract for an important client. It was more detailed than those she'd worked on in the past and she became anxious that she couldn't do it.

Then she tried thinking of the contract as a cluster of terms and agreements, with which she was already familiar. Looking at the contract like this, Nina was able to work through each item with confidence.

Exercise - Avoiding Over-Analysis

Which examples describe actions you can take to avoid over-analysis in high-pressure situations?

Options:

1 - You commit to finishing the proposal by the end of next Monday.

2 - You decide to submit your proposal since it's good enough, if not perfect.

3 - You divide the quarterly report into an assessment of each of the five departments, completing each one before moving on to the next.

4 - You list each alternative approach you considered for the budget review in case your boss condemns
the one you chose.

5 - You detail the tasks involved in your review of company policies to ensure your success.

Answer:

Option 1: This option is correct. Setting a time limit for what needs to be done is an effective way to move from analysis to action.

Option 2: This option is correct. Aiming for progress and not perfection is important to ensure continued output, especially if you have a tendency to overanalyze.

Option 3: This option is correct. Breaking a complicated task into more manageable tasks is effective for avoiding over-analysis.

Option 4: This option is incorrect. To avoid over-analysis, you should focus on what you do, rather than on what you could, would, or should do.

Option 5: This option is incorrect. You should instead stay focused on what you're trying to achieve, rather than on the details of your performance.

Correct Answer(s):

1 - You commit to finishing the proposal by the end of next Monday.

2 - You decide to submit your proposal since it's good enough, if not perfect.

3 - You divide the quarterly report into an assessment of each of the five departments, completing each one before moving on to the next.

Overconfidence is the second tendency that some people have in high-pressure scenarios. Having a sense of confidence about yourself and your abilities is important. However, overconfidence can lead to failure.

The Negative Side of Overconfidence

Overconfidence leads people to underestimate challenges and fail to ask whether their skills, experience, and knowledge are sufficient to accomplish the task at hand. An example of an overconfident response is refusing to consider alternatives to opinions and decisions.

Because overconfident employees may act brashly, the consequences of their actions can be more damaging than those caused by overthinking. This is because their mistakes tend to be more elaborate, and so require far more time and effort to resolve.

Arrogance, if left unchecked, can lead to complacency. For example, you may become convinced that you no longer make trivial mistakes. Such a mindset makes it easy for you to miss simple errors in your work.

Overconfidence can prevent you from seeking the help you may require to meet a given objective or achieve a set standard. This can lead you to repeat mistakes or get behind in your work.

Results of Overconfidence

Just as overthinking results in too much attention being paid to the possibility of failure, overconfidence often leads to too much focus on the expected rewards of success. In both cases, your focus is drawn away from the task at hand, and directed to the outcome of the situation instead.

Take Dwayne, for example. He was recently promoted to the position of editor at a publishing house. Given an important manuscript as his first task, he began to go through it, not only making corrections, but also rewriting large sections that he felt were poorly researched and argued. Dwayne thought he'd been given too easy a task to begin with, but that he'd improved it with his superior understanding of the subject matter.

While working on the manuscript, Dwayne was offered help by experienced editors who remembered being bogged down by their first projects. But Dwayne refused assistance. He was so convinced of his skills that Dwayne felt he didn't need help to impress his superiors.

However, when the manuscript's author read Dwayne's changes, he was offended. Dwayne hadn't realized that the author was an expert in the field and that his own grasp of the material was elementary in contrast to the author. He was so focused on his own ability and ambition to impress that he didn't bother to check who the author was.

Controlling Overconfidence

You can use several techniques to avoid overconfidence in high-pressure situations. First, stay humble and accountable. Second, understand that good decision-making requires you to know your limits. Third, make sure that you learn from your previous mistakes. Fourth, be realistic about the time and effort needed to complete tasks. And fifth, make it a habit to think ahead.

Stay Humble and Accountable

To guard against overconfidence, make an effort to stay humble and accountable. Consider Mark, who quickly completed what he thought was a routine budget analysis. However, his results differed from those expected.

Rather than assume he was correct, he noted the disparity, and asked a coworker for help. By admitting that he'd underestimated the challenge, they solved the problem together, and Mark learned to be more careful in the future.

Know Your Limits

Good decision-making requires that you know the limits of your abilities and your knowledge. For example, once doubtful of his team's solution, Brian reluctantly admitted he didn't share their technical understanding of the issue.

Instead of arguing with them and asserting his authority, Brian asked his team to help him understand the issue. In this way, they reached an effective solution together.

Learn from Your Previous Mistakes

When things go wrong, it's important to analyze what went wrong and why so you can learn from your mistakes. As an example, a few weeks ago, Susan made a scheduling error that resulted in several missed deadlines.

Though she'd been doing the scheduling for years, Susan took the time to recognize how the problem occurred. Then she created a checklist that included what she learned so she wouldn't repeat the same mistake.

Be Realistic About Time and Effort

Underestimating challenges can lead to costly errors. Aim to be realistic about the time and effort required for a task to avoid this.

Take Thomas, who needed to update an office's computer systems. Though he'd done similar jobs in the past, he still took care to budget his time realistically. Thomas gave himself extra time, which enabled him to solve an unforeseen problem while staying on schedule.

Thinking Ahead

Thinking ahead and asking what might go wrong is a helpful way to avoid errors due to overconfidence. For example, Luanne was leading a team of accountants through an important audit of a company. She began by considering what potential problems could arise.

What if she were to lose any of her staff during this busy time? To ensure that work wouldn't be lost in such a scenario, she compiled a list of consultants that she could hire if this happened.

Exercise - Avoid Being Overconfident

Which examples describe effective ways to avoid being overconfident in high-pressure situations?

Options:

1 - You recognize that the figures you've been given may be flawed and distort your findings.

2 - You think you'll be able to complete a routine task in four days, but allow yourself a week in case of unexpected delays.

3 - You plan to consult an expert on an area which you're somewhat, but not completely, familiar with.

4 - You reaffirm that a mistake was made, but that you weren't to blame for your involvement 5. You move forward from mistakes by forgetting about them and focusing on success.

Answer:

Option 1: This option is correct. Thinking ahead about potential problems is a good way to keep yourself from acting overconfidently under pressure.

Option 2: This option is correct. Being realistic about time and effort required is an important way to stave off overconfident tendencies.

Option 3: This option is correct. Understanding your limits and acknowledging the need for help is important for guarding against overconfidence.

Option 4: This option is incorrect. Part of avoiding overconfidence is being accountable when mistakes are made, and being humble.

Option 5: This option is incorrect. It's important that you learn from your mistakes so as not to repeat them. This is a good way to keep from being overconfident.

Correct Answer(s):

1 - You recognize that the figures you've been given may be flawed and distort your findings.

2 - You think you'll be able to complete a routine task in four days, but allow yourself a week in case of unexpected delays.

3. You plan to consult an expert on an area which you're somewhat, but not completely, familiar with.

Avoiding Overthinking and Overconfidence

When under pressure, people may tend to overthink the situation, or react with overconfidence. Each type of behavior has undesirable results.

To avoid overthinking situations, you should try to stay focused on what you're doing and just do what you do. Remember to strive for progress and not perfection, and try to set a time limit for what needs to be done. Finally, try to break tasks into smaller ones that are more manageable.

To resist the potentially damaging consequences of overconfidence, stay humble and accountable. Remember that good decision-making requires that you understand your limits. Make an effort to learn from your previous mistakes and stay realistic about the time and effort a task will take. Finally, get into the habit of thinking ahead about what may go wrong, and plan for these possibilities.

To Conclude

When under pressure, people may tend to overthink the situation, or react with overconfidence. Each type of behavior has undesirable results.

To avoid overthinking situations, you should try to stay focused on what you're doing and just do what you do. Remember to strive for progress and not perfection, and try to set a time limit for what needs to be done. Finally, try to break tasks into smaller ones that are more manageable.

To resist the potentially damaging consequences of overconfidence, stay humble and accountable. Remember that good decision-making requires that you understand your limits. Make an effort to learn from your previous mistakes and stay realistic about the time and effort a task will take. Finally, get into the habit of thinking ahead about what may go wrong, and plan for these possibilities.

To use this tool, begin identifying a task that you're struggling with, and read the list of statements often related to overthinking. Then, put a check next to those that apply to your current task. Finally, write statements that counter those that apply to you. You can print this table in a word processing or spreadsheet application and use it to complete this activity.

1. Think of a particular task or assignment that you're under pressure to complete, and are spending too much time on, then review the statements. Place a checkmark next to each statement that describes why you're taking too long to complete the task.

2. For each item that you checked, write a sentence that counters it. For example, if you checked the statement "I require the inspiration of last-minute panic to complete things," your countering sentence could be "I can complete things in advance of deadlines."

If your selections are more nuanced, you should think about yourself a little more. For example, if you selected "I'm always having trouble saying that 'I'm finished; with anything," you might say "I'm going to make an effort to change my tendency to fail to complete things."

Overthinking Tasks

Statements	Apply to Me	My Statements	Countering
It needs to be perfect			
I'm putting off the decision so I don't make the wrong one			
I have a hard time moving from planning things to doing them			
This task is keeping me from one I'd rather postpone anyway			
I need the inspiration of last-minute panic to complete things			
My ambition is consumed by fits of "What ifs"			
I like to keep myself occupied with this task so I don't find myself with nothing to do			
I'm meticulous and need to refine each detail sufficiently			
I always have trouble saying "I'm finished" with tasks			
I'm afraid of facing criticism for something I've said was			

finished

Use this job aid to help you revise your automatic thoughts in order to optimize your perception of a situation when you're under pressure.

Thought distortions can affect your performance, especially when you're under pressure. Use this table as an aid to recognize if and how your thoughts are being affected by pressure, and determine how you can revise them if necessary.

Distorsion Type	Example	Revised thought
All or nothing	"I can't do anything right."	"I did make a minor mistake, but it's been corrected, and I learned a valuable lesson from it."
Negative bias	"I don't think we'll ever catch back up."	"We've had a small setback, but if we all share the workload, we should be back on track by next week."
Emotive reasoning	"My boss undermines all of	"I have no reason to believe

	my efforts."	this is true, and I should take his comments as opportunities for improvement."
Exaggeration	"I'll lose the account because of this mistake."	"It's too early to tell if I've made a mistake, but even if I have, it's not going to be as costly as I've made it out to be."
Blame	"Her poor performance caused the fall in quarterly sales."	"While we all played a role in the drop, some aspects are beyond our control."

Consider Alfred, a technology researcher with an electronics company. His boss asked him to give a presentation about his current research to the company's executive board. Whether Alfred sees this as an exciting opportunity or as an incitement of anxiety largely depends on how he deals with pressured situations.

Automatic Thoughts

The stress you feel in a situation can be influenced by how you interpret the situation. When you perceive a situation negatively, you may perform below your ability. To help you perceive a situation more clearly, you can follow a four-step method. First, notice automatic thoughts. Second, identify distortions. Third, question whether there's evidence for these thoughts. And fourth, revise these thoughts, and apply more constructive interpretations.

Notice Automatic Thoughts

The first step is to notice automatic thoughts. If your thoughts are untrue, negative, or contrary to your best interests, they may have negative consequences. Many thoughts are unconscious and automatic. These thoughts can produce physiological responses — such as hypertension and hyperventilation — that can make you more susceptible to negative reactions. Learning to recognize how thoughts are distorted can help improve your performance under pressure.

For example, if you're convinced that your teammate is subverting your performance, you're likely to waste energy looking for evidence of this instead of focusing on doing your best work.

Identify Distorsions

The second step for improving how you look at a situation is to identify distortions. There are several types of thought distortion that often occur when you're under pressure.

First is the tendency to view situations in terms of all or nothing, through overgeneralization. Second is having a negative bias. Third is being prone to emotive reasoning. Fourth is engaging in exaggeration. And fifth is the tendency to wrongly place blame on others, or on yourself.

All or Nothing

All or nothing thinking is characterized by thinking in terms of absolutes, such as "always," "never," or "every," or "none." This thinking can make situations seem hopeless.

For example, Jesse's boss told him and his team that their deadline had been moved up a week. Jesse's immediate reaction was that they'd never get the project done on time while fulfilling their other commitments.

They'd have to drop everything and focus on this one task, but fail to deliver their other tasks on time.

By viewing the moved deadline as so burdensome and impossible, Jesse kept himself from finding a way to pull everyone together to succeed.

Negative Bias

A negative bias shifts your focus to the negative, excluding the positive, and leads you to assume the worst in cases when it isn't warranted.

Brian, for instance, is vying for a promotion. He spent a week preparing for a meeting where he planned to pitch an idea as part of his bid for the new role. During the meeting, one of Brian's colleagues asked a question that exposed a potential weakness that Brian hadn't considered. Following the meeting, Brian sat at his desk, brooding over the question and convincing himself that his coworker was trying to block his promotion.

Brian's negative bias took over his thought process, which might otherwise have taken the comment as constructive and an opportunity for improvement.

Emotive reasoning

Emotive reasoning occurs when you base your interpretation of a situation on emotions.

Consider Julia, who had been waiting for a colleague to finish his portion of a report so she could add her analysis. When he was late passing it along to Julia, she reasoned that her coworker was trying to sabotage her by making it difficult for her to deliver the report to their boss on time.

Julia's emotions of anger and suspicion created this conclusion and kept her from offering help or another solution.

Exaggeration

Exaggeration distorts your perception of situations because you inflate the significance of the negative and disregard other factors.

Take Nicholas, who recently submitted a draft of an important project to his boss. His boss returned the work and said it was very good, but thought that Nicholas should use less technical vocabulary. Nicholas began to think that his boss was telling him that he didn't have what it takes to move from a technical role to higher-management roles. He felt that he had failed in this instance and wouldn't receive another opportunity.

Exaggeration kept Nicholas from listening to the compliment his boss was giving him, and made him focus instead on the small criticism.

Blame

Blame involves accepting responsibility for something that wasn't your fault, or attributing it to others, without good reason.

Take Marsha, for example. When her team's proposal for a lucrative marketing contract was rejected, rather than consider which of the client's needs weren't met by their proposal, she immediately accepted the blame and believed that if she had only tried harder, they would've succeeded.

By doing so, Marsha wasn't able to take anything productive from the situation and remained committed to accepting the blame and resisting future leadership.

Unreasonable Beliefs

Unreasonable beliefs can lead to distorted thoughts. For this reason, the third step of reaching optimal perception is to question whether there is evidence for these thoughts, or if they're the result of irrational thoughts.

81

A good example of this is emotive reasoning, where conclusions tend to follow emotions such as suspicion or anger and have little basis in objective reality.

So if you think your boss hates you, you should ask yourself why you think this. If there's no objective proof for it, you should dispel the thought.

Exercise - Understanding Thought Distorsion

Match each example of a thought to the type of thought distortion involved.

Options:

A - "I can't do anything right."

B - "I don't think we'll ever catch back up."

C - "My boss undermines all of my efforts."

D - "I'll lose the account for this small mistake."

E - "Her poor performance caused the fall in quarterly sales."

Targets:

1 - All or nothing.

2 - Negative bias.

3 - Emotive reasoning.

4 - Exaggeration.

5 - Blame.

Answer:

An all or nothing distortion causes you to generalize outcomes into absolutes – for example, thinking that you can't do anything right.

A negative bias makes you focus on the negative aspects of a scenario, like never being able to catch up, even if it's possible.

Reasoning based on emotions assumes things that are felt, regardless of whether they're true or not, like your boss undermining you.

When the negative aspects of a situation are exaggerated, it's often to the point where the situation seems hopeless – like a minor mistake having grave consequences, for example.

This thought distortion is when responsibility for a situation is either wrongly assumed by an individual or attributed to others – for example, attributing a decrease in an entire quarter's figures to one individual's sales.

Correct answer(s):
Target 1 = Option A
Target 2 = Option B
Target 3 = Option C
Target 4 = Option D
Target 5 = Option E

Revise YourThoughts

The fourth step for achieving optimal perception under pressure is to revise your thoughts, and apply more constructive interpretations of them. To do this, try using more positive words. You should also explore whether there are reasons for your thoughts, and whether there might be alternative explanations.

Consider the statement, "There's no way we'll get everything done on time." Revised, it might read, "We've got a lot to do, but I'm confident we can get it done if we each take on one extra task this week."

Exercise - Revising Thoughts

Match each negative statement with its revised counterpart.

Options:
A - "I can't do anything right."
B - "I don't think we'll ever catch up after this."
C - "My boss undermines all my efforts."

D - "I'll lose the account for this mistake."

E - "Her poor performance caused the fall in quarterly sales."

Targets:

1 - "I did make a mistake, but it's been corrected, and I learned a valuable lesson from it."

2 - "We've had a small setback, but if we all share the workload, we should be back on track by next week."

3 - "I have no reason to believe this, and I should take his comments as opportunities for improvement."

4 - "It's too early to tell if I've made a mistake, but even if I have, it's not as bad as I've made it out to be."

5 - "While we all played a role in the drop, some aspects are beyond our control."

Answer:

In this revision, not being able to do something right is recognized as not being wholly negative, and a lesson is drawn from it. The revision notes that the setback isn't grave, and proposes sharing the work as a solution.

The lack of evidence for an undermining boss is noted, and his comments are interpreted in a more positive light. This revision questions whether there a mistake has been made, and puts it into perspective, that it's not as bad as was thought.

The blame for the low sales is shared, and the fact that some factors are beyond your control is noted.

Correct answer(s):

Target 1 = Option A

Target 2 = Option B

Target 3 = Option C

Target 4 = Option D

Target 5 = Option E

Under pressure, responses to situations are often emotional and based on automatic thoughts. These include having a negative bias, blame, emotive reasoning, and exaggeration. To begin taking appropriate action in the face of pressure, you need to recognize what exactly the challenge is, and distinguish between automatic thoughts and emotional reactions.

Recognize the Challenge

The next step is to determine what exactly needs to be accomplished. This allows you to minimize emotional distractions and focus on dealing with the situation. Finally, this clarifies your priorities and, when others are involved, helps to establish a common understanding of the issue.

Take Alan, for example, a salesman at an online advertising agency. He's been missing his sales targets lately and is facing pressure to improve his performance. During the last week of a sales period, Alan still hasn't reached his target. In response to this pressure, Alan's thoughts are being distorted by his negative bias, blame, emotive reasoning, and exaggeration.

Negative Bias

Alan thinks he's struggling because he's unlikable. He can't make sales because his personality simply turns his customers off before he can make his pitch. Following this train of thought, Alan's sales continue to decline.

Blame

Alan shows his frustration by blaming himself for being a poor salesman, and blaming his boss for not providing him with adequate training. Alan is very upset about this by the time his performance review arrives, and he confronts his boss about his lack of training.

Emotive Reasoning

Alan feels that he hasn't been trained properly. He thinks this is because his colleagues see him as a lost cause. Alan imagines that the other salesmen think that he'll never succeed as a salesman, but they aren't able to be honest with him. Alan figures that they're simply humoring him until finally he becomes frustrated and quits.

Exaggeration

Alan's sales aren't as bad as he thinks. But his train of thought allows him to believe that something is fundamentally wrong, leading to a host of negative conclusions.

It would be a great help for Alan to consider how the real challenge before him is being colored by his emotions and automatic thoughts. By stripping away these emotional hooks, Alan would recognize that what he needs to accomplish is an increase in his sales. Reducing his emotional distractions would help him focus on improvement — such as seeking the training he feels he needs – which could also increase his confidence.

Exercise - Identifying a Challenge

Alex is a graphic designer at a publishing company. At a meeting to finalize the design of a book that he's been working on for several weeks, his boss tells him that she's unhappy with the way it looks and that Alex should have a revised version to her by the end of the week.

Alex feels that apart from when his boss gave him some very rough guidelines of what she wanted when assigning the task, she hasn't been present and remains unaware of the project's challenges. Nor does she seem to be aware of Alex's other projects, which don't allow him the time to redesign the book. After the meeting, Alex speaks to a colleague who had a similar experience. Alex begins to think this is a case of their boss needing to exert power over the creative teams.

Which reactions effectively address the real problem of the situation?

Options:

1 - "I'll schedule a meeting with my boss to discuss her specific expectations for the book."

2   "I'll speak with my boss about clearing time from my schedule so I can address this issue."

3 - "I need to tell my boss that I'm not the only one frustrated with how she treats the talent around here."

4 - "I need to tell one of the executives about how my boss wields her authority."

5 - "I'll just have to tell my boss that I don't know what else to do to make her happy."

Answer:

Option 1: This option is correct. The real challenge here is for Alex to meet his boss's expectations, which need to be clarified before he can meet them.

Option 2: This option is correct. Because Alex's boss may not be aware of his other commitments, it's important for Alex to ensure that each task is given due attention. This may include enlisting help, or having the deadline for something postponed.

Option 3: This option is incorrect. Exaggerating his and a colleague's frustration contributes nothing to Alex's challenge. Instead, Alex should strip these hooks away from the real issue – the design of the book.

Option 4: This option is incorrect. Emotive reasoning, such as Alex's boss exerting her authority, clouds the issue that needs attention – the redesign of the book.

Option 5: This option is incorrect. A negative bias highlights the worst aspects of a situation to make that situation seem impossible, leaving little room for solutions.

Correct answer(s):

1 - "I'll schedule a meeting with my boss to discuss her specific expectations for the book."

2 - "I'll speak with my boss about clearing time from my schedule so I can address this issue."

To Conclude

Stressful situations tend to distort how a situation is perceived. There are four steps you can follow to optimize your perception of situations.

First, notice your automatic thoughts. These thoughts often arise from emotional reactions to situations and may go undetected at first. Second, identify thought distortions. Common types of thought distortions include having a negative bias, blame, emotive reasoning, and exaggeration.

The third step is to question whether there is any evidence for this kind of thinking. The fourth step is to revise your thoughts. This involves restating them in a more positive way, by separating them from any emotional or automatic thinking.

To take action in high pressure situations, you need to first make sure you've optimized how you look at the challenge. This means asking whether your perception may be distorted by emotion and revising any thoughts that are obscured. Then you should clarify what the real challenge is.

The Effective Action Method

When you have a clear idea of the challenge, you can follow a four-step method to take effective action. The first step is to question the challenge. The second step is to identify your goal. The third step is to generate and evaluate possible solutions. And the fourth step is to design an action plan.

The first step of the method, **question the challenge**, involves asking questions that focus on the challenge. For example, ask yourself, "How urgent is it?" This prompts you to **consider a timeline** for dealing with the issue at hand.

You should also ask "How much time do I have to address it?" Only by **establishing the urgency** of a problem and the time that's available can you evaluate how best to resolve the challenge.

Finally, ask "What additional information do I need to be able to respond to it?" This ensures that you **have a detailed understanding of the problem** before taking action.

Consider Ralph, an engineer managing a project to build a dam. A couple of weeks before submitting the plans, Ralph learns from the development agency that the budget has shrunk by a significant margin.

Ralph is frustrated because this agency has previously miscalculated budgets, leaving others in his position to find a solution. Ralph decides that he needs to address this problem before the design is submitted.

Ralph begins by making sure to keep the challenge in perspective. He notes that he has roughly one week to deal with this urgent issue, and may need to consult experts for technical information.

Exercise - Defining the Challenge

You're a systems analyst at a technical support company. Recently, the software you set up has been causing some problems. You've been approached by several employees experiencing difficulties, which seem to be escalating.

Which examples illustrate things you should do as part of the first step in the process of taking action?

Options:

1 - Assess how damaging the problem is.

2 - Determine how soon the malfunctioning software needs to be repaired.

3 - Speak to people from each area experiencing difficulties.

4 - Consider enlisting an external specialist.

5 - List each set of repairs needed.

Answer:

Option 1: This option is correct. Part of the first step is to determine the urgency of the issue – in this case, what damage is being done.

Option 2: This option is correct. The first step requires you to get an idea about how much time you have to solve the problem.

Option 3: This option is correct. Part of the first step is asking what additional information you may need to respond effectively – in this case, asking about the variety of problems being experienced.

Option 4: This option is incorrect. Proposing solutions, such as getting outside help, isn't part of the first step.

Option 5: This option is incorrect. Determining what needs to be done to solve the problem isn't part of the first step.

Correct answer(s):

1 - Assess how damaging the problem is.

2 - Determine how soon the malfunctioning software needs to be repaired.

3 - Speak to people from each area experiencing difficulties

The second step of the method for taking action is to identify your goal. To help identify it, ask "What do I need to achieve?" You need to be clear about the challenge, and what kind of solution is acceptable, before you can prescribe any actions.

Remember Ralph? His second step is to ask himself what he needs to achieve to address the funding problem. He decides that he needs to keep the project running on schedule. This goal is directly related to the challenge, and avoids any emotional or automatic thoughts.

Exercise - Identify Your Goal

You're an accountant working for a large oil and gas company. Due to cutbacks, there are fewer people in your role trying to keep up with the same amount of work, and you're under constant pressure to keep up. When your boss tells you that he needs you to take on yet another account, you become angry and desperate.

Which examples represent goals that address what needs to be achieved?

Options:

1 - Your boss needs to realize that he doesn't understand that the organization is making unrealistic demands of its accountants.

2 - You need to hire an assistant to help you accomplish everything being asked of you.

3 - You need to meet with your boss to plan a schedule that allows you to meet each of your objectives.

4 - You need to scan your projects to ensure that your tasks are limited to those requiring your expertise, and that tasks that can be accomplished by lower-level employees are so delegated

Answer:

Option 1: This option is incorrect. Recognizing what needs to be achieved means setting realistic and achievable goals that are free from emotional hooks. This goal stems from frustration and anger.

Option 2: This option is incorrect. Hiring an assistant is an unrealistic reaction stemming from frustration. Recognizing what needs to be accomplished means choosing actions that are reasonable and free from emotional hooks.

Option 3: This option is correct. This goal is realistic and achievable. What's more, it allows you to voice your concerns of overwork.

Option 4: This option is correct. This goal is reasonable because it takes the particulars of the scenario into account and has the potential to resolve the problem at hand.

Correct answer(s):

3 - You need to meet with your boss to plan a schedule that allows you to meet each of your objectives

4 - You need to scan your projects to ensure that your tasks are limited to those requiring your expertise, and that tasks that can be accomplished by lower-level employees are so delegated

Once you've defined your challenge and identified your goal, the third step is to generate and evaluate possible solutions. This involves thinking about what kind of actions you could take and the effects they may have. You can begin by imagining a variety of alternative solutions to the problem.

Generating Solutions

Then try to think of any potential negative effects. You may also want to discuss solutions with a colleague or mentor. For example, perhaps you're thinking of how to manage a difficult customer. Having an experienced colleague evaluate your solutions may be helpful.

Finally, select the best solution from your list. This may be the one that's most practical, or that offers the most advantages and fewest drawbacks.

Evaluating Potential Solutions

Considering a variety of solutions increases the value of the action you ultimately decide on. This is because it not only allows you to think about what else you could've done, but also provides you with a clear rationale for your decision.

Ralph considers potential solutions. He thinks he could appeal to the funding agency to renegotiate the project budget. Alternatively, he could ask the other engineers for ways to reduce the construction costs. Or he could stay the course and hope that if he does go overbudget, the agency will be forced to cover the extra costs.

Ralph thinks that the first option is unlikely, since the agency isn't known for loosening budgetary constraints. Similarly, if he doesn't redesign the project, it will almost certainly exceed the revised budget, which will have serious consequences.

Ralph decides that he should meet with his team of specialists to find options for reducing the cost of the project.

Exercise - Generating and Evaluating Solutions

Blanche is a writer at a magazine. She hasn't been able to confirm several quotations she plans to include as part of her story and her deadline is drawing near.

Which actions are appropriate for the third step of the method?

Options:

1 - Suggest changing the focus of the story to highlight her confirmed research.

2 - Consider that if she keeps the story as it is, and the unchecked quotations are discovered, she could lose her job.

3 - Ask another journalist to have a look at her options.

4 - Ask to have her deadline extended.

5 - Ask what kind of result is acceptable to her.

6 - Ask herself when she'll have to make her decision.

Answer:

Option 1: This option is correct. Part of the third step is to select the most acceptable solution of those proposed and evaluated.

Option 2: This option is correct. An integral part of the third step is to evaluate potential solutions, trying to think of any potential negative effects.

Option 3: This option is correct. In the third step, it's a good idea to discuss options with a colleague or mentor to gain another perspective on the issue.

Option 4: This option is incorrect. The first part of the third step is to imagine alternative solutions so that they can be compared with each other. Having her deadline extended, however, doesn't address the problem that her sources haven't been corroborated.

Option 5: This option is incorrect. Asking this question is part of the second step, identifying the goal. In the third step, the focus should be on generating solutions and evaluating them.

Option 6: This option is incorrect. Determining how much time there is to deal with the challenge is part of the first step. In the third step, she should generate and evaluate potential solutions.

Correct answer(s):

1 - Suggest changing the focus of the story to highlight her confirmed research.

2 - Consider that if she keeps the story as it is, and the unchecked quotations are discovered, she
could lose her job.

3. Ask another journalist to have a look at her options

Once you've decided on a solution, the final step is to design a plan of action to implement the solution you've chosen. The first thing you should do is divide what needs to be done into manageable tasks or steps that can be accomplished with relative ease. This can help to keep you from being overwhelmed by the pressure, or becoming paralyzed by over-analysis.

Planning Your Actions

When you have a manageable set of tasks prepared, you should then assign specific times to them. This helps keep you committed, and stops you from spending too much time on any one task. Ensure that one item on your action plan can be done immediately to build momentum. This should be something that you can do as soon as you finish writing your action plan.

This is important because if you don't include something you can do right away, you're more likely to fall prey to procrastination.

To meet his goal of redesigning the dam in order to stay on schedule, Ralph puts together a plan of action. He plans to begin by contacting his team of engineers by e-mail to explain the situation and arrange a meeting. Ralph wants to begin with this step so he can take immediate action and build momentum toward achieving his goal.

Next, he'll consult a materials expert to discuss his options. Ralph will also consult a local engineer from the region where the work is being done to come up with ways to save money, such as hiring local labor. Finally, he'll prepare a new design and have it reviewed by his superior to ensure its accuracy. He schedules each of these steps to be completed within three days so a meeting can take place at the end of the week.

Exercise - Design a Plan of Action

Stacey is a web designer. Her current project is more complex than projects she's had in the past. Her goal is to achieve the same standard of excellence that has come to characterize her work.

What actions should Stacey perform in the fourth step of the method?

Options:

1 - Break the project into having a meeting with the client, doing research for the project, sketching a design, and programming the site.

2 - Make a schedule of times for the tasks she has broken the project into.

3 - Start by e-mailing the client to book a time to meet.

4 - Decide how long she can spend designing the web site.

5 - Ask herself what sort of outcome will satisfy her in the long run.

Answer:

Option 1: This option is correct. Dividing what has to be done into manageable tasks will help Stacey to keep moving from one task to the next and avoid paralysis.

Option 2: This option is correct. Assigning specific times to each task guards against perfectionism and procrastination.

Option 3: This option is correct. It's helpful to include one task that can be done immediately. In this case, e-mailing the client will allow Stacey to build momentum toward her goal right away.

Option 4: This option is incorrect. Determining how much time you have to meet a challenge is part of the first step. The fourth step focuses on dividing the task into smaller tasks and assigning times to complete them.

Option 5: This option is incorrect. This is something done as part of the second step. In the fourth step, the focus is on dividing the task into manageable jobs and scheduling times for them.

Correct answer(s):

1 - Break the project into having a meeting with the client, doing research for the project, sketching a design, and programming the site.

2 - Make a schedule of times for the tasks she has broken the project into.

3 - Start by e-mailing the client to book a time to meet.

Exercise - A Strategy Under Presure

What are the benefits associated with having a strategy to take action while under pressure?

Options:

1 - You can respond more effectively to the situation.
2 - Your chosen solution's value is enhanced.
3 - You're less likely to be overwhelmed by the pressure.
4 - You're less likely to fall prey to procrastination.
5 - Your successful performance is assured.
6 - You'll be able to avoid the consequences of pressure.

Answer:

Option 1: This option is correct. When you have a clear idea of the challenge, your response is likely to be more effective.

Option 2: This option is correct. Considering and weighing alternative solutions increases the value of a solution. This is because it benefits from having been selected from a variety of alternatives.

Option 3: This option is correct. Dividing your task into manageable tasks helps guard against becoming paralyzed by over-analysis.

Option 4: This option is correct. Including something that you can do immediately allows you to build momentum toward achieving your goal. This guards against procrastination.

Option 5: This option is incorrect. Having a strategy in place for managing high-pressure situations can help you to perform more effectively. But it doesn't guarantee success.

Option 6: This option is incorrect. High-pressure situations are nearly inevitable in business environments. However, it is valuable to have a strategy in place for managing your performance when they arise.

Correct answer(s):

1 - You can respond more effectively to the situation.
2 - Your chosen solution's value is enhanced.

3 - You're less likely to be overwhelmed by the pressure.

4 - You're less likely to fall prey to procrastination.

Exercise - Taking Action Under Pressure

You're an architect and your first drafts of drawings for a new project have been returned to you. Apparently they failed to live up to what the developer had envisioned.

Match the examples of your actions with the corresponding steps of the method for taking action in a high-pressure situation.

Options:

A - You clarify that your drawings are needed as soon as possible B. You aim to have your drawings reflect the developer's vision.

C - You recognize that asking others for help will disrupt schedules D. You intend to begin by revisiting the developer's vision.

Targets:

1 - Question the challenge.

2 - Identify your goal.

3 - Generate and evaluate possible solutions.

4 - Design an action plan.

Answer:

The first step involves clarifying the details of the challenge, including how much time you have to address it. The second step is to state your goal — for example, to reflect the developer's vision in your work.

The third step requires you to imagine different solutions and evaluate them. In this case, asking others for help is rejected because it will disrupt their schedules.

The fourth step is to design a plan of action. Reviewing the developer's vision is an example of how the plan should include a task that can be done immediately to build momentum.

Correct answer(s):
Target 1 = Option A
Target 2 = Option B
Target 3 = Option C
Target 4 = Option D

To Conclude

There's a **four-step method** you can follow for taking action in high-pressure situations. First, question the challenge. This involves asking how urgent the challenge is, how much time you have to address it, and what, if any, additional information you need to be able to respond to it.

The second step is to identify your goal. This can be accomplished by asking yourself what you need to achieve.

The third step is to generate and evaluate possible solutions. Here you should imagine alternative solutions, think of any potential negative effects they may have, discuss them with a colleague or mentor, and finally select the most acceptable one.

The fourth step is to design a plan of action. Begin by dividing what needs to be done into manageable tasks, and assign specific times for accomplishing each. Finally, make sure that one element can be done immediately to build momentum toward your goal.

CHAPTER FOUR
Practice Managing Pressure

Use this job aid to help you take action to perform effectively in high-pressure situations.

Having a strategy in place for taking action under pressure can help you to perform more effectively. Use the table to review the steps of the process and the actions associated with each step.

Step	Action
1. Question the challenge	Ask: How urgent is it? How much time do I have to address it? What additional information do I need to be able to respond to it?
2. Identify your goal	Ask: What do I need to achieve?
3. Generate and evaluate possible solutions	Imagine alternative solutions Think of potential negative effects of proposed solutions Discuss proposed solutions with a

4. Design an action plan

colleague or mentor Select the most acceptable solution

Divide what has to be done into manageable tasks Assign specific times for accomplishing these tasks
Make sure one element can be done immediately to build momentum

You work in the Ordering Department at a company that manufactures and ships office furniture. You've worked there for ten years and have become familiar with the processes, finding your own shortcuts.

Recently, however, new software has been installed to ensure that each ordering specialist is following the same protocol, requiring you to relearn the entire system.

When you learned about this change, you became frustrated, thinking that management never thinks about what effects these kinds of changes will have on the people who have to use them. Later, as you're struggling to adjust to the new system, you feel that that you'll never get it and since you're simply unable to work with computers. Finally, you begin to see the initiative as a way for management to coax employees who are uncomfortable working with new technology into quitting.

You're a web content manager for a large hotel chain. Today you're scheduled to attend three important meetings. Between them, you need to finish the new reservation system you've been designing for the past two months so that it can be submitted by the end of the day, and go live by the end of the month.

The first meeting runs over schedule by 45 minutes. From the beginning of it, you recognized that far too many points were being addressed for the meeting to finish on time, which angered you immediately. With only an hour until your next meeting, you stayed upset while you had a quick lunch on the run, and failed to get to the reservation system task.

The next meeting similarly ran over the scheduled time and left only another small window before the third meeting. At this rate, it became impossible for you to accomplish everything you needed to accomplish.

In your opinion, meetings that run over their allotted time are inconsiderate and indicative of poor organization. In the last instance, you wondered if the delay was on purpose because you've been at odds with the meeting leader lately.

You're a recruitment manager for a company that publishes university textbooks. In order to fulfill several new contracts, your department has recently agreed to increase its output by a significant margin over the next three years. You've been put in charge of hiring ten new employees, who will work with the existing staff to meet the increased quota. They need to be given three weeks' training, so they must be hired within a month.

After advertising the vacancies to recent graduates, you review the résumés you've received and feel that of the 200 applicants, only five are worth even inviting for an interview. You panic because you're left with only two weeks to hire enough people. You think that students simply aren't being educated to the standard that you and your peers were. You feel your company must not have adequately researched the availability of qualified recent graduates before agreeing to the new contracts, and that it has put this pressure on you.

You're the distribution manager for an online clothing retailer. Your company wants to obtain exclusive online distribution rights from a prestigious luxury brand. You're meant to attend a meeting with one of your organization's founders and executive directors to propose the details of the deal to representatives of the brand.

A few days before the meeting, however, you learn that you'll be the sole representative of your company due to a scheduling conflict. Your initial reaction was enthusiastic, seeing it as a chance to showcase your skills. However, you soon felt the pressure this put on you, and started to doubt your negotiation skills, convincing yourself that you won't be able to close the deal on your own. You began to wonder what, if any, future you might have at the company if you fail to secure this account.

CHAPTER FIVE

Achieving Relational Performance Under Pressure

For the vast majority of people, work involves interaction with others, which means that good working relationships are indispensable to good performance. But pressure is also an inescapable aspect of work, and pressure can cause relationships to suffer.

Before turning to the potential of pressure to damage relationships, consider the five features that really good working relationships share. These are trust, openness, a sense of interrelatedness – the ability to perceive the connections between your tasks and those of your colleagues, respect for one another, and effective communication.

Trust

Trust is emotional and logical. Emotionally, you may expose your vulnerabilities to people, trusting that they won't take advantage of you. Logically, you can objectively assess the situation, and conclude that you can trust someone to behave in a predictable manner.

For example, you can place trust in colleagues by seeking input from them. You can also demonstrate trust if you're comfortable discussing your successes and failures with colleagues. If you're a manager, you could demonstrate trust by allowing others to work without unnecessary oversight.

Openness

Openness can mean different things in different contexts. It can mean honesty, or openness to new experiences. In the workplace, you can demonstrate openness by being open to new ideas and being able to adjust your responses to current circumstances.

For example, an open colleague will actively listen to others, and not reject ideas without careful consideration. Healthy debate among colleagues and talking freely about current challenges are signs of an open environment.

Sense of Interrelatedness

A sense of interrelatedness is about an awareness of the bigger picture. For example, if you have this quality, you can see how your current activities relate to organizational goals.

Interrelatedness is also an awareness of how your job role affects the performance of others. For example, say you're a sales representative dealing with customers. If you're efficient, you create less work for the customer service team dealing with complaints.

Respect

Respect for others is absolutely essential – regardless of the context. In the workplace, respect can be demonstrated by being considerate, truthful, and tactful with colleagues.

115

Examples of showing respect in the workplace are listening attentively to colleagues at meetings and being constructive and tactful when giving feedback.

Effective Communication

Effective communication is understanding when it's appropriate to communicate in person, by e-mail, or by phone.

For example, it's appropriate to use face-to-face communication for sensitive matters such as performance reviews. For routine communication that must be recorded, say meeting minutes, e-mail is the more appropriate option.

Exercise - Characteristics of Good Relationships

Which actions exemplify the characteristics of good working relationships?

Options:

1 - You seek the opinion of a colleague to narrow a performance gap.

2 - You carefully consider the opinion of a colleague that's opposite to your opinion.

3 - You're going to be slightly delayed with a deliverable, so you telephone a colleague who's waiting on the information.

4 - You criticize a colleague's incompetence in a team meeting.

5 - You provide your manager with a verbal summary of a team meeting that he missed.

Answer:

Option 1: This option is correct. Seeking the opinion of others demonstrates trust. All performance discussions should be in confidence.

Option 2: This option is correct. Careful consideration of a colleague's opinion is a sign of openness to new ideas. You may still end up disagreeing, and that is fine, but it's important to consider alternative opinions.

Option 3: This option is correct. Awareness of the impact of activities on others is an example of interrelatedness. It's appropriate to make colleagues aware of time challenges as soon as possible.

Option 4: This option is incorrect. Although issues should be discussed openly, it's disrespectful to openly criticize a colleague. Constructive feedback in a tactful manner is preferable.

Option 5: This option is incorrect. Verbal communication is inappropriate for routine matters such as meeting minutes. An e-mail would be more appropriate.

Correct answer(s):

1 - You seek the opinion of a colleague to narrow a performance gap.

2 - You carefully consider the opinion of a colleague that's opposite to your opinion.

3 - You're going to be slightly delayed with a deliverable, so you telephone a colleague who's waiting on the information.

Pressure isn't always bad. In fact, some pressure is desirable; it generates action. In some circumstances it enhances performance — like an athlete getting psyched up for a race. In the workplace, pressure can bring members of a team closer, focusing the team on a common objective and producing feelings of camaraderie when all are sharing the same pressures. However, it's important to understand how pressure can have negative impacts.

The Negative Side

Consider Lawrence. He's a client service executive in a logistics company. The company promises delivery of packages within 48 hours. Due to poor weather conditions, many packages have been delayed, and call volumes from customers have increased ten-fold. The majority are complaints, and some customers have become agitated.

Lawrence's manager is out of the office, so in frustration he asks a colleague, Hilary, to help take calls. Hilary tells him that she has important tasks to complete, and is concerned that she hasn't received appropriate training for dealing with difficult clients.

Lawrence is annoyed and dismisses her fears. He tells her that it's a unique situation, and it should be prioritized over Hilary's tasks.

Lawrence's in a high-pressure situation. Preoccupied with his own priorities, he is insensitive to Hilary's. He doesn't take time to ask Hilary about her workload, or consult a superior for direction. The way he dismisses her concerns indicates he wasn't really listening to Hilary. He is allowing the pressure he's under to damage their working relationship.

Pressure can affect the quality of perceptions, especially when emotions run high. An individual experiencing pressure will often display less awareness of others, and become over-focused on the current issue. In some cases, the individual may compromise professionalism and show insensitivity toward colleagues. Other possible negative effects are diminished communication and diminished collaboration.

Less Awareness of Others

Pressure can cause you to become excessively focused on your own problem – such as a deadline you're struggling to meet. And this can lessen your awareness of others around you.

For example, with the intention of getting a job done quickly and correctly, individuals may fail to be aware of the pressures others are under.

Code Insensitivity

Increased pressure may compromise professionalism. People can drop their guard, and be less sensitive to others in the heat of the moment. This may result in a lack of respect and verbal aggression.

Colleagues will inevitably suffer from the poorly managed pressure. For example, if an individual feels pressure from a superior, the frustration may result in insensitivity to the feelings of others. The individual may snap at a colleague, or be offhand with a customer.

Diminished Communication

High-pressure situations can lead to diminished communication. The most common communication barrier in teams is ambiguity. Team members may be busy and therefore not take time to ensure everyone understands the team's goals and procedures.

For example, a team leader could assign an immediate and important task to a team, taking for granted that everyone will work well together. However, some team members may react negatively to the pressure. Perhaps a team member isolated himself, preferring to work alone. Another colleague could show visible signs of stress such as becoming flustered and agitated.

Diminished Collaboration

High-pressure situations can lead to diminished collaboration. When under pressure, some individuals may become secretive, suspicious, or reluctant to take risks due to fear and anxiety. This is particularly problematic when there's an existing lack of trust and openness in a team.

Diminished collaboration can lead to a lack of efficiency and productivity. For example, poor information sharing can lead to lost work time because two team members are unknowingly duplicating work. Diminished collaboration can also lead to delayed decision-making, reduced quality, and poor commitment and effort.

Consider Paul, who works on the payment reconciliation team in a bank. His team is undergoing a compliance review and he's trying to manage his daily tasks, in addition to managing the frequent information requests from the legal team.

Paul's manager has advised the team that it'll have to work through lunch. A team member, Sarah, quietly pulls Paul aside and confides that she's got a prior appointment that she can't change. She asks Paul to cover for her. Paul feels unable to say no. He reluctantly agrees.

Paul struggles with his own tasks, and he realizes that he doesn't have the resources to complete Sarah's tasks. Colleagues are starting to ask questions, and Paul's angry that he's spending more time lying to confused colleagues about why Sarah's temporarily unavailable. He snaps at the legal administrator assigned to his team, saying Sarah can deal with issues when she bothers to come back.

Exercise - Reaction in High-Pressure Situations

Which statements correctly describe Paul's reaction to the high-pressure situation?

Options:

1 - Paul's frustrated that he has to lie to colleagues about where Sarah is, and that it has created confusion.

2 - Paul was insensitive by voicing his frustration with Sarah in front of the legal administrator.

3 - Paul was being very sensitive to Sarah's personal priorities and acted like a team player,

4 - Paul avoided asking Sarah what her appointment was for; he needs to know why he should prioritize her work.

5 - Paul showed a lack of communication by neglecting to ask anyone for the resources to complete Sarah's tasks.

Answer:

Option 1: This option is correct. Diminished collaboration is common in pressured situations. It often manifests in secretive and suspicious behavior.

Option 2: This option is correct. People can often be insensitive in high-pressure situations. Often, verbal aggression is directed at a colleague when an issue isn't dealt with in a tactful manner.

Option 3: This option is incorrect. Instead of trying to help out his colleague Sarah, Paul should have tactfully suggested she raise the issue with their manager.

Option 4: This option is incorrect. Sarah's appointment is a personal matter, and she should discuss it with their manager so that her task can be reallocated fairly.

Option 5: This option is correct. Diminished communication is common in pressured situations. Paul should have raised his concerns with Sarah or a superior.

Correct answer(s):

1 - Paul's frustrated that he has to lie to colleagues about where Sarah is, and that it has created confusion.

2 - Paul was insensitive by voicing his frustration with Sarah in front of the legal administrator.

5. Paul showed a lack of communication by neglecting to ask anyone for the resources to complete Sarah's tasks.

An individual's response to pressure may be rooted in that individual's work style. Of course, a preference for one style doesn't mean an individual won't adopt another style under different circumstances. Furthermore, an individual's response to pressure situations will vary depending on his or her ability to cope with different kinds of pressure.

Work Styles

There are four work styles: expressives, drivers, amiables and analysts. Expressives tend to be assertive and socially engaging, while drivers are assertive yet more results-focused than people-focused. Amiables are usually sociable, cooperative and empathetic toward others. Finally, analysts are often very methodical and display perfectionist behavior.

Expressives

Expressives are emotional and assertive. They enjoy action, and tend to thrive on being in the limelight. They therefore love being center stage and seek out eye-catching projects.

Expressives prefer the stimulus of other people to working alone. They're interpersonally proactive, and relate easily and effortlessly to strangers. As a result, a person of this outgoing style tends to have a larger circle of acquaintances than those with other styles.

Drivers

Drivers are very practical and results-focused. They're characterized by decisiveness. Due to a typical impatience, drivers normally like to lead in shared tasks or projects.

Drivers typically excel at time management. They love setting high, yet realistic, objectives for themselves and others. Drivers usually don't take direction well.

Amiables

Amiables tend to be supportive, cooperative, and have empathy for colleagues. Amiables are team players, and can focus more on everyone getting along than getting the job done. In this respect, they prefer to work with others and solve their problems.

Amiables don't seek the spotlight and seldom get into ego clashes with others. Amiables are less likely than the more assertive styles to seek power for themselves. They can be skilled at encouraging others to expand on their ideas and are good at seeing value in other people's contributions.

Analysts

Analysts are usually quiet and less emotional than others styles. They're perfectionists and will take as much time as necessary to get the job done 100% right. They therefore set very high standards and strive to excel.

Analysts are critical thinkers, and sticklers for detail. They take pride in attention to detail. Their exacting standards cause them to be generally very sparing with compliments and expressions of appreciation.

Exercise - Work Styles

Match each person's situation to the appropriate work style.

Options:

A. Sophie's a sales executive. She loves the constant energy and enjoys being assertive. She relates effortlessly to strangers.

B. Violet's a client services representative. She loves helping people resolve their problems.

C. Antonio is a team leader in a leading bank. He's known to make decisions very quickly and be hard on his team to deliver results.

D. Luther is a finance manager. He's well organized and excels at building processes that produce outstanding results.

Targets:

1 - Expressive.

2 - Amiable.

3 - Driver.

4 - Analyst.

Answer:

A high level of assertiveness and an ability to relate well to new people are characteristics of expressives, such as Sophie.

The desire to help others resolve problems is a characteristic of amiables, such as Violet.

Decisiveness and being results-driven are characteristics of drivers, such as Antonio.

Being well organized and process-driven to a high standard are characteristics of analysts, such as Luther.

Correct answer(s):
Target 1 = Option A
Target 2 = Option B
Target 3 = Option C
Target 4 = Option D

Individual Style Preference

An individual's style preference can become a comfort zone when under pressure. Adopting these mechanisms — or behaviors — isn't a conscious choice; it's automatic. When under pressure, the behavior exhibited by each style often becomes more extreme.

Reactions under pressure are related to an individual's level of assertiveness and responsiveness. Expressives, being both assertive and emotional, may go on the offensive and lash out in anger. Drivers may become dictatorial, given the high level of assertiveness and lack of responsiveness. Amiables may become acquiescent, or docile, given the lack of assertiveness and desire to please everyone. Analysts may become detached to avoid emotional involvement due to their low assertiveness and responsiveness.

Expressives

Consider Sophie, the expressive sales executive. Her manager has insisted she drastically improve her sales in the next three months. As an expressive, she's likely to lose her temper with her manager, or redirect her frustration by complaining openly to colleagues.

Drivers

Consider Antonio, the team leader in a bank. When under pressure to meet a project deadline, he's likely to become impatient and dictatorial with his team members to get the tasks completed on time.

Amiables

Consider Violet, the amiable client services representative. When put under pressure by an agitated client call, she's likely to become acquiescent in an effort to appease the customer. She's in danger of overcommitting to requests in an effort to please. However, an assertive approach would more likely resolve the issue in a timely and efficient manner.

Analysts

Consider Luther, the finance administrator with the analyst work style. When under pressure to produce a report quickly, he's likely to avoid conflict and discussion. Instead, he'll take as much time as necessary to get the job done right.

Unfortunately, while these automatic mechanisms are instinctive ways of dealing with pressure, they can have a negative impact on others. If people are unaware of their reactions under pressure, they're unlikely to change.

In such circumstances, people do things in an extreme way without thinking through the consequences.

Exercise - Responses and Work Style

Match the responses to pressure to work style types.

Options:

A - Gabriel has an emotional outburst when a client criticizes his proposal.

B - Brian becomes impatient and insists Polly completes a report from the beginning.

C - Sally won't commit to a solution between two colleagues who are debating aggressively.

D - Alice misses deadlines, as she's always striving for perfection.

Targets:

1 - Expressives.

2 - Drivers.

3 - Amiables.

4 - Analysts.

Answer:

Gabriel's emotional outburst is a common reaction of expressives when under pressure. This is due to a high level of assertiveness and responsiveness.

Brian's impatience and being dictatorial are characteristics of drivers under pressure. This is due to a high level of assertiveness, but low responsiveness.

Sally being acquiescent is characteristic of amiables, due to low assertiveness and high responsiveness.

Alice being a perfectionist is characteristic of analysts. Perfectionists have extremely high accuracy targets.

Correct answer(s):

Target 1 = Option A

Target 2 = Option B

Target 3 = Option C

To Conclude

Good working relationships are characterized by trust, openness, interrelatedness, respect, and effective communication. Pressure, however, can cause individuals to react negatively, and compromise good working relationships.

Pressure can reduce awareness of others, sensitivity to others, communication, and collaboration. These effects can be made more extreme depending on the work styles of the individuals under pressure.

The four work styles are expressives, drivers, amiables, and analysts. Under pressure, expressives can go on the offensive, drivers can become dictatorial, amiables may become acquiescent, and analysts may become excessively detached from others.

There are four work styles, and people typically react differently under pressure depending on their style.

Work Style	Descriptions	Reaction under Pressure
Expressives	Usually socially engaging and have a high level of assertiveness coupled with responsiveness. They love being center stage and seek out eye-catching projects. Prefer the stimulus of other people to working alone. They're interpersonally proactive, and relate easily and effortlessly to strangers.	Expressives, being both assertive and emotional, may go on the offensive and lash out in anger.
Drivers	Very practical and results-focused. They're characterized by decisiveness.	Drivers may become dictatorial given their high level of assertiveness and lack

	Due to a typical impatience, drivers normally like to lead in shared tasks or projects. Typically excel at time management. They love setting high, yet realistic, objectives for themselves and others. Drivers usually don't take direction well.	of responsiveness.
Amiables	Tend to be supportive, cooperative, and have empathy for colleagues. They're team players, and focus more on everyone getting along than getting the job done. They don't seek the spotlight and seldom get into ego clashes with others. Less likely than the more assertive styles to seek power for themselves. They can be skilled at encouraging others to expand on their ideas and are good at seeing value in other people's contributions.	Amiables may become acquiescent, or docile, given their lack of assertiveness and desire to please everyone.
Analysts	Usually quiet and less emotional than others styles. They're perfectionists and will take as much time as necessary to get the job done	Analysts can avoid emotional involvement due to their low assertiveness and responsiveness.

131

right. They therefore set very high standards and strive to excel.

Critical thinkers and sticklers for detail. They take pride in attention to detail. Their exacting standards cause them to be generally very sparing with compliments and expressions of appreciation.

In order to perform effectively with others who are under pressure in the workplace, you must manage your own reactions to pressure. If you don't manage your reactions to pressure well, you may fall into a trap of negative interactions with others. For example, in a stressful situation, you may become irritable, tactless, or uncooperative toward colleagues.

Manage Stressful Situations

In order to manage pressurized situations, you must first identify what you can control and what you can't control. What you can control is yourself and your own reactions, and what you can't control is other peoples' reactions. But in order to be in control of your reactions you need to avoid being overwhelmed by emotion. Aim to be rational and in control of your responses to pressure.

You may have noted that the first thing you need to do is recognize when you're stressed. This is the first step in managing your reactions in a high-pressure situation. Unless you can spot the signs of stress in yourself, you can't begin to take control. It's important to examine the emotion associated with your reaction to uncover its true source. Finally, you must act to take control of your emotions, and modify your behavior accordingly.

Recognize Strtess

Recognizing when you're stressed can be challenging because everyone is unique, so your stress responses will likely be different from those of your work colleagues. Furthermore, it's sometimes harder to self-reflect and recognize our own stress responses.

There are many ways that people react under pressure. For example, some people will react with anger, frustration, or fear. The signs of stress may be explicit, such as a verbal outburst. Or they may be implicit, such as impatience, restlessness, or even illness.

Other people may react by becoming quiet, withdrawn, or even overly agreeable.

Stress Clues

There are clues that can help you recognize that you're under stress. Physical symptoms include fatigue, an increased heart rate, high blood pressure, and feeling hot and clammy. Breathing can become short and labored. Many people flush easily, whereas others become pale. Psychological and emotional symptoms include distorted thoughts, panic, impatience, and distress. Such symptoms will inevitably impair your ability to be rational and objective. This can therefore compromise your ability to handle complex tasks.

Consider Regina, she's been working late most evenings on a project. Frequently she comes home tired and becomes impatient with her family. Friends often tell her she looks stressed. She often feels inadequate about her performance, and insecure in her job.

Regina decides to keep a journal to determine what's causing her to feel stressed. For a period of two weeks, she takes ten minutes at the end of each day to record her thoughts. In one column she writes down her activities and interactions at work. In the second column she writes down how it makes her feel.

At the end of the two-week period, Regina reviews the journal to identify any trends. She realizes that her greatest feelings of fear occur on Tuesdays when she has team meetings and must present project updates to her manager. She also realizes her feelings of fear are because she hasn't discussed her performance with her manager.

Exercise - Stress Symptoms

What were Regina's stress symptoms?

Options:

1 - Fatigue.

2 - Withdrawn.

3 - Impatience at home.

4 - Job insecurity.

5 - Overly agreeable.

Answer:

Option 1: This option is correct. Regina experienced the physical symptom of frequent tiredness.

Option 2: This option is incorrect. Regina's stress response manifested in impatience at home.

Option 3: This option is correct. Regina's impatience at home was a psychological symptom of stress.

Option 4: This option is correct. Regina fears for her job, which is a psychological sign of stress.

Option 5: This option is incorrect. There is no evidence that Regina was afraid of her manager and acting overly agreeable.

Correct answer(s):

1 - Fatigue.

3 - Impatience at home.

4 - Job insecurity.

Examine Your Emotions

The second step in managing your reactions to stress is to examine your emotions. To do this, you should ask yourself relevant questions:

- What's making me frustrated?
- Why am I so anxious about this situation?
- Can feelings of anger help me achieve a resolution?
- How do I want to appear to my coworkers?
- Can I communicate effectively with my coworkers if I'm emotional?

Remember Regina? Now that she's identified her reactions to stressful interactions in work, she adds a third column to her journal. For each stressor, Regina asks herself a number of questions to examine her emotions more closely. For example, she asks herself why she fears presenting her project updates, and what's making her so worried about her job security. She also asks herself if her colleagues think she's tired and stressed.

Exercise - Examining Emotions

Did Regina take appropriate steps to examine her emotions?

Options:

1 - Yes.

2 - No.

Answer:

Regina is following the second step for managing her reactions to stress. She's taking a structured approach and asking herself some challenging questions.

Correct answer(s):

1. Yes

Managing Your Reaction

The third step in managing your reactions to stress is to take control of your emotions. After asking yourself why you're feeling stressed, try to step back from the emotion and calmly address the situation. For example, if you get upset at work, say by a rude customer, stop and think – step out of the emotional situation.

Being able to recognize physical, psychological, and emotional stress responses doesn't mean that you won't experience strong emotions. But what it does do is help you control your emotions instead of letting them control you.

If you're upset, ask yourself what was upsetting about the situation. Then consider its importance. Often, people blow small events out of proportion. Even if the situation was important, your reaction should be focused on solutions, rather than emotional reactions. If you can't focus on how you can make things better, at least avoid making things worse.

A big part of taking control of your emotions is changing variables. For example, ask yourself if the same situation would upset other people you know. Pay attention to how you feel about the situation after looking at it from different perspectives.

Questions to Ask Yourself

- Ask yourself these questions to help you change the variables of a situation:
- Was it really the situation that caused you to feel this way, or your interpretation of it?
- If a different person was involved, would it upset you as much?
- If the event happened at a different time, would it be as upsetting?
- If you had certain people or resources around, would that change your emotional reaction? Would the same event or situation cause a similar reaction from other people you know?

Remember Regina? She's now ready to take control of her emotional reactions to pressure at work. For example, the following Tuesday she decides to address her job security fears with her manager.

In addition to her project updates, Regina has updated her performance review documents. At the end of her meeting with her manager, she gives him the documents, and asks him if they can review them together the following week.

Regina feels empowered because she's been proactive and taken steps to ensure her manager addresses her concerns about her performance at work.

Exercise - Three Step Technique to Manage Your Reactions

Match the activities to the related stage of the three-step technique for managing reactions to stress.

Options:

A - Notice if you feel flushed and distracted when you need to present to a large audience.

B - Ask yourself if feelings of anger help handle a personality conflict with a colleague.

C - Determine if it's your manager's behavior that upset you, or your interpretation of his behavior.

Targets:

1 - Recognize when you're stressed.

2 - Examine your emotions.

3 - Take control of your emotions.

Answer:

Identifying physical symptoms and behaviors is an example of recognizing when you're stressed.

This is the kind of question you can ask yourself to help you examine your emotions in a stressful situation.

Questioning your behavior and interpretation of events is an example of changing the variables to take control of your emotions.

Correct answer(s):

Target 1 = Option A

Target 2 = Option B

Target 3 = Option C

One of the most difficult interpersonal challenges in the workplace is dealing constructively with other people when they're reacting to stress. There are guidelines to help you deal with such situations. First, always show respect to others. Second, learn to detect stress in others. Third, avoid getting hooked by the other person's behavior. And last, don't try to block a person from using their automatic stress-reducing mechanisms.

Everyone Wants to be Treated with Respect

Consider respect, the first guideline to managing reactions to pressure. Can you think of some ways you can demonstrate respect to colleagues? You may have suggested getting the basics right, such as being polite and courteous. Everyone wants to be treated with respect at work. You can show colleagues respect through your actions toward them. For example, listening is an important skill that demonstrates respect. That is, you should listen attentively to what others have to say without speaking over them.

Another way to show colleagues respect is to use their ideas to improve processes and procedures. Of course, it's important that you give the appropriate credit, or even encourage the person to implement the idea. Wherever possible, you should encourage coworkers to express their opinions and ideas.

Avoid Inappropriate Actions

Avoid actions that could indicate disrespect, such as making disparaging comments or nit-picking. Although healthy debate and constructive criticism are good for important topics, don't constantly criticize colleagues over little things. Furthermore, never belittle, judge, or patronize others. It's advisable to praise much more frequently than you criticize.

Another behavior to avoid is reacting negatively to colleagues — for example mirroring their negative behaviors. Negative reactions can reinforce stress-induced behavior.

Example - Negative Reactions

Consider Noah, a client services executive. He's in a meeting, and his colleague Sally is giving him reasons for why she hasn't contributed to a joint project. Follow along as Noah and Sally discuss the issue.

Sally: I'm really busy with this important client! If I don't respond to him immediately, he threatens to withdraw his business! He always asks for me personally, so I'm finding it hard to focus on anything else.

Noah: Sally, you really have to learn how to multi-task! He's not the only client you know. There's a 24-hour service level agreement, so just tell him that!

Sally: But, what I mean is, I've been told by my manager to really look after him. He's our top client...

Noah: I'm sure you'll think of something. Anyway, I need you to complete the report by the end of the week. You're not the only one who has important tasks.
Sally: Cathy could help out. She's free to do some work on that report... Sally is thoughtful
Noah: It's your responsibility. Noah is dismissive.
Sally: I'll do the best I can, Noah. Sally is unhappy.

In this example, Noah failed to show Sally respect. When she tried to explain that she was dealing with her top client, he showed he wasn't really listening by interrupting her in a dismissive way. Furthermore, he didn't use her idea of calling on Cathy's help.

Noah should've stayed calm and listened attentively to her concerns. He should've avoided any negative reactions, and instead encouraged Sally to be proactive and search for a positive solution to her situation.

Exercise - The Appropriate Responses

Your colleague Mike is under pressure to meet a deadline. He tells you he'll be late delivering a report because of another priority. You need the report urgently, and you're frustrated as it's the third time this month the report is late.

What are appropriate responses to Mike?

Options:

1 - "I understand you're under pressure. Is there anything I can do to help?"

2 - "OK. When you've dealt with this issue, I'd love your help in finding ways to streamline the workload."

3 - "I need that report urgently, Mike. Can you please get it to me ASAP?"

4 - "This is typical, Mike! You've been late twice this month already. You need to manage your time better."

Answer:

Option 1: This option is correct. Although you needed the report urgently, you were polite and avoided reacting negatively to Mike.

Option 2: This option is correct. Instead of disparaging Mike, you encouraged him to express opinions and ideas for improving workflow.

Option 3: This option is incorrect. Your choice of response only adds to Mike's feeling of pressure.

Option 4: This option is incorrect. It's not appropriate to disparage or nit-pick when a colleague's under pressure.

Correct answer(s):

1 - "I understand you're under pressure. Is there anything I can do to help?"

2 - "OK. When you've dealt with this issue, I'd love your help in finding ways to streamline the workload."

The second guideline to help you deal with stressed colleagues is detecting their stress. It's helpful to know colleagues' work styles because reactions under pressure are related to assertiveness and responsiveness. For example, expressives, being both assertive and emotional, may become angry. Or, amiables may become docile, given their lack of assertiveness and desire to please.

Identifying Emotional States

When trying to detect stress responses in others, behaviors are usually more obvious from the more overtly assertive styles — expressives and drivers. However, with analysts and especially amiables, it can be harder to recognize the subtle differences between normal and reactive behavior.

When detecting stress in colleagues, try to identify their emotional states. You can do this by listening carefully to what they say and how they say it. You can gather clues from how they respond to external events such as someone greeting them or asking them to do something.

144

For example, if under pressure, their style-based behavior may become more extreme or more rigid.

Learning to Recognize the Signs

Having spent a lot of time with colleagues, you should learn to note specific signs of stress in their behavior. For example, your manager is an expressive and he frequently becomes agitated with you when the team doesn't meet its deadlines. A typical behavior that indicates stress is demonstrative body language, for example pointing, visible tiredness, or a defensive body position.

It's beneficial to think about your colleagues' feelings. Ask yourself how their behavior makes you feel. For example, when your manager's agitated, do you feel guilty? Being able to identify that the behavior is related to stress can help you deal with it better. For example, instead of feeling guilty, you can choose not to take the reaction personally.

Remember Sally and Noah? There are many ways that Noah could've identified Sally's emotional state to improve his reaction toward her. Her body language indicated she's an expressive, as she was waving her arms around as she spoke.

Sally's tone of voice indicated that she was upset. It was high pitched and she spoke very quickly. Sally also expressed fear of losing the client.

Exercise - Detecting Stress

What are examples of ways to detect stress in colleagues?

Options:

1 - Pay attention to your colleague's body language.

2 - Notice if a colleague becomes very quiet and withdrawn when faced with making a presentation.

3 - Solicit advice from colleagues on whether this is a good time to present an idea to your manager.

4 - Observe how your manager reacts to a stressed individual and mirror your manager's behavior.

5 - Determine that a colleague is being overly excited and melodramatic

Answer:

Option 1: This option is correct. For instance, if your colleague seems unusually tired it may be an indicator of stress.

Option 2: This option is correct. Noting specific behaviors in colleagues can help you detect when they become stressed, such as when giving a presentation.

Option 3: This option is incorrect. Relying on third-hand information isn't an appropriate way to detect stress in others.

Option 4: This option is incorrect. Mirroring the behavior of others is not an appropriate way to detect stress in others.

Option 5: This option is correct. Identifying someone's emotional state can help you respond calmly, and more positively toward the person.

Correct answer(s):

1. Pay attention to your colleague's body language

2. Notice if a colleague becomes very quiet and withdrawn when faced with making a presentation

5. Determine that a colleague is being overly excited and melodramatic

The third guideline to help you deal with stressed colleagues is to avoid getting hooked by their stressed behavior. One way to do this is to reframe your thinking. For example, rather than focusing on your dislike of the behavior the other is exhibiting, realize what lies behind it. You'll generally find that the person has experienced an enormous buildup of pressure that's causing them to react in this way.

Showing Empathy

Another way of avoiding getting hooked is to try to show empathy for what a person's trying to cope with. Imagine yourself in that person's shoes. You can also remind yourself that you're not the real target of the other person's behavior — whether the behavior is lashing out or avoidance. The behavior's a response to a stressor, and you happen to be in the way. So it's best not to take it personally.

Consider Jack, he manages a small team of banking administrators. Beth, one of the team members, is upset because she's under pressure to complete a task. Follow along as Jack deals with Beth's behavior.

Beth: Jack, you asked me to reconcile the debtors report by end of today, but I'm already overstretched with my daily tasks.

Jack: I'm glad you came to me to clarify. You should focus on the debtor report for today.

Beth: But I'm also covering for Marie's holidays! Did you forget? Beth is sarcastic.

Jack: I didn't forget Beth. I understand that you're under pressure with a lot of competing tasks. It's hard to know what to prioritize. I'll reassign your other duties.

Beth: OK then! Thanks for clearing that up. Beth is happy.

In this example, Jack avoided getting hooked on Beth's behavior by remaining calm rather than reacting to her agitated behavior. He reacted positively, therefore refraining from adding to her stress.

Jack showed empathy toward her task management challenges and didn't take her sarcasm personally.

Exercise - The Most Appropriate Response

You're on the phone with a client that your team manages. She's agitated and frequently uses phrases such as "you didn't send the report on time" or "you should've asked me first." Although you deal with the client regularly, the whole team has different responsibilities.

What's the most appropriate response?

Options:

1 - Avoid taking offense at her comments, and instead seek ways to resolve the client's issues promptly.

2 - Advise her that it wasn't your fault and transfer her to another colleague before she can complain further.

3 - Ask her which of your colleagues she dealt with on these issues, as she must have you confused with someone else

Answer:

Option 1: This is the correct option. It's best to avoid taking her comments personally, otherwise you may become hooked on her negative behavior.

Option 2: This option is incorrect. Avoiding responsibility and transferring her to a colleague unnecessarily is likely to add to her negative behavior.

Option 3: This option is incorrect. Challenging the client for the benefit of blaming someone else will likely add to her negative behavior.

Correct answer(s):

1 - Avoid taking offense at her comments, and instead seek ways to resolve the client's issues promptly.

The fourth guideline to help you deal with stressed colleagues is to avoid blocking automatic stress-reducing mechanisms. If you do this — say, you tell someone to calm down — you're more likely to prolong the stress reaction.

Built-In Mechanisms

Consider Steven. He's frustrated with a colleague's outburst and tells her to "pull herself together." Although it's tempting to try to intervene with someone's stress responses, such a reaction only adds to the person's stress.

Unfortunately, there's a strong tendency to urge people not to use their stress behavior. For example, Mike has an analytic style and he's stressed and has become withdrawn. If you want to know what's on his mind, you might be tempted to tell him to "just get it off his chest." However, this well-meant advice merely adds to his stress.

Of course, when someone uses such behavior over a long period of time, the situation must be dealt with. If this needs to be done, wait until the person is no longer stressed before addressing the issue. You can then help him or her develop tactics to prevent the buildup of too much stress.

Exercise - The Appropriate Response

You're training a new colleague, Lucy. Your organization has a mandatory test at the end of new hire training. Lucy is worried about the test, as she's having difficulty understanding some of the company's banking processes. Although she started the training bright and cheerful, she's become pale and tired looking by the end of the first week. She's been asking you a lot of questions, which you feel are obvious and repetitive.

What's an appropriate response to Lucy's behavior?

Options:

1 - Listen carefully to her questions and make sure she fully understands your answers. Also recognize that her tiredness is likely due to working hard for the test.

2 - Recognize that asking lots of questions is a process that Lucy uses to learn, and exercise more patience.

3 - Tell Lucy that she shouldn't bother you with the little things. She should be able to figure them out for herself.

4 - Reassure Lucy that the test isn't a big deal. Only you will see the results so she's getting worked up over nothing.

5 - Don't assume that your training skills are inadequate. Instead ask Lucy for feedback on how she feels she's progressing.

Answer:

Option 1: This option is correct. You've shown respect by listening to Lucy and avoiding criticism. You've also detected her stress responses by noting specific behaviors she exhibits.

Option 2: This option is correct. You've avoided getting hooked on Lucy's behavior by reframing your thinking. You also haven't gotten in the way of her stress-reducing mechanism.

Option 3: This option is incorrect. It's inappropriate to criticize Lucy for asking lots of questions when it's your job to train her.

Option 4: This option is incorrect. It's inappropriate to trivialize the test. It's your job to make sure she's prepared, so she'll be capable when she starts work.

Option 5: This option is correct. It's important not to take Lucy's reaction personally and assume you've failed to train her adequately.

Correct answer(s):

1 - Listen carefully to her questions and make sure she fully understands your answers. Also recognize that her tiredness is likely due to working hard for the test.

2 - Recognize that asking lots of questions is a process that Lucy uses to learn, and exercise more patience.

5 - Don't assume that your training skills are inadequate. Instead ask Lucy for feedback on how she feels she's progressing.

To Conclude

When dealing with high-pressure situations, there's a three-step technique to help you manage your reactions. First, recognize when you're stressed. Then examine the source of your emotional reaction to the situation. Finally, you can take control of your emotions, and modify your behavior accordingly.

It can be more difficult when dealing constructively with other people when they're reacting to stress. However, there are some guidelines to help you deal with such situations. First, always show respect to others. Second, try to detect when others are under pressure or reacting to stress. Third, avoid getting hooked by the other person's behavior. Last, don't try to prevent people from using their automatic stress-reducing mechanisms.

Use this follow-on activity to help you ask the right questions about pressurized situations in the workplace.
Think of a challenging situation you recently faced when working with others under pressure.

Question	Answer
Describe the situation	
What was upsetting about the situation?	
Are you still upset about it? If so, how long have your feelings persisted?	
Do you feel that you can resolve the situation in your current emotional state?	

Would the same event or situation cause a similar reaction from other people you know?

Now, take the same event and explain it from another person's point of view. For example, a colleague that was involved, or your manager.

Use this job aid to help you be effective in dealing with others under pressure.

Dealing with others under pressure

Steps	Descriptions
Show respect	Listen attentively Avail of their ideas Don't criticize Avoid reacting negatively
Detect stress in others	Identify their emotional states Note specific behaviors Think about their feelings
Avoid getting hooked	Reframe your thinking Realize what lies behind the stress Show empathy Don't personalize the situation
Don't interfere with automatic stress-reducing mechanisms	Allow others to respond in their own way to stress

Performance Under Pressure

Unpleasant interactions with colleagues are a typical source of pressure in the workplace. It's likely that you have encountered a situation recently that you wish you'd handled differently. Even if you have exceptional people skills, you'll still come across challenging people in the work environment from time to time — whether it's a colleague, superior, or client.

Challenging Interactions

Stressful interactions come in many forms. For example, you might encounter non-contributors — team members who don't do their fair share. Or you may have indecisive clients blaming you for an error or miscommunication. Another familiar example would be overcritical coworkers, or coworkers who makes unreasonable demands on your time. Such pressures usually build over time.

Reacting negatively to colleagues in pressure situations can be damaging to work relationships. Typical reactions include becoming irritable, actively avoiding people, or being hypercritical. Or you may find you're losing your sense of humor. In pressure situations, the preferred action is to remain calm, professional, and deal with the issue assertively.

Consider Amy and Ellen. They're colleagues working in the same building but on different floors. Ellen has promised Amy a report, but it's two days late. Amy needs to contribute to the report and present it to her manager in two days. In previous circumstances, she's had to go ahead and complete Ellen's section of the report in order to meet her deadline.

Amy has already sent Ellen a gently worded e-mail as a reminder, and left two voicemails on her phone. She sees Ellen in the canteen, so she confronts her there.

Amy is irritated and tells Ellen that she doesn't contribute her fair share of the work, and that avoiding her e-mails and voicemails is unprofessional. This is a pressure situation that resulted in Amy reacting negatively toward Ellen.

Exercise - Reaction for the Situation

Consider Ryan, a client services executive in a bank. Ryan faces a challenging situation with Keith, a coworker. Over the last month, Keith has made a couple of errors on a client account, and has blamed Ryan for the errors. Furthermore, Keith frequently pesters Ryan to help him complete his work, yet criticizes and trivializes Ryan's priorities.

Ryan feels uncomfortable confronting Keith, as he's popular, witty, and well liked by management. Instead, Ryan steers clear of Keith where possible and tries to keep all interactions strictly work-related.

How has Ryan reacted to the situation with Keith?

Options:

1 - Ryan's reaction to Keith was negative. By actively avoiding Keith, he's not addressing the problem.

2 - Ryan's reaction to Keith was positive. He chose to control his anger toward Keith's negative behavior.

3 - Ryan's reaction to Keith was positive. It's best to keep all interactions work-related to avoid negativity.

Answer:

Option 1: This is the correct option. Avoidance is a negative reaction to pressure situations. Addressing the issue in a calm and professional manner is to be preferred.

Option 2: This option is incorrect. Ryan doesn't genuinely control his anger. Instead, he uses the negative tactic of avoidance because he is unable to confront Keith.

Option 3: This option is incorrect. Keeping interactions strictly work-related is negative because a problem exists between these workers that needs to be addressed.

Correct answer(s):

1. Ryan's reaction to Keith was negative. By actively avoiding Keith, he's not addressing the problem.

You can use a four-step technique to help you manage negative interactions at work. First, monitor your feelings and tendencies toward instinctive responses to pressure. Then, use a diversion – such as a brisk walk – to avoid obsessing about the situation. Next, replace negative thoughts with positive thoughts. Finally, prepare to interact positively.

Identify Automatic Responses

So the first step is to identify your own automatic responses when faced with a difficult interaction with a colleague. Is your first instinct to shout at him, to appease him, or to avoid him?

It helps to consider past experiences – either with the relevant colleague, or similar situations with someone else. Recall your instinctive reactions. Keeping a record can give you a better sense of your instinctive reactions to pressure situations.

By considering past experiences, you can get an idea of the consequences of reacting instinctively.

Consider Gail. She deals with a difficult client by telephone on a bi-weekly basis. The client can be indecisive, and frequently changes time frames and deliverables. Gail finds herself frustrated, challenging him on agreed details, and the conversations frequently become repetitive.

In an effort to improve her working relationship with the client, she proactively takes notes of all telephone conversations. In the notes section of the client account, she details all client concerns, what was discussed, and agreed time frames for deliverables. She then e-mails a copy to the client.

In addition to the formal notes on the client account, Gail carefully considers her reactions to the client's demands, and how she could have behaved differently. She then updates her performance plan on a weekly basis, detailing her areas for improvement.

Exercise - Monitoring Negative Feelings

Did Gail appropriately monitor her negative feelings toward her client?

Options:

1 - Yes, recording her thoughts and feelings was the most appropriate way to monitor her feelings and tendency to challenge the client.

2 - Yes, Gail took proactive steps to prevent the meetings from becoming repetitive by e-mailing the client details of what was agreed.

3 - No, it would've been more appropriate if Gail had first addressed the issue with the client. Keeping notes is an example of avoiding the issue.

Answer:

Option 1: This is the correct option. When managing your performance with others under pressure, it's important to identify your automatic responses, review previous experiences, and understand the implications of your actions.

Option 2: This option is incorrect. Taking detailed notes is good practice, but it's not an example of monitoring feelings and tendencies to react negatively.

Option 3: This option is incorrect. In order to effectively manage your interactions with others, identify your automatic responses, review previous experiences, and understand the implications of your actions before confronting the individual.

Correct answer(s):

1. Yes, recording her thoughts and feelings was the most appropriate way to monitor her feelings and tendency to challenge the client.

In this situation, Gail took a proactive approach to monitoring the situation. She recorded the details of the interaction, and her feelings and reactions to the client's difficult behavior.

The benefit of monitoring feelings and tendencies toward negative reactions is increased self-awareness. If you're not aware of your own feelings and tendencies, you're more likely to become unsympathetic to others.

Consequently, relationships can disintegrate further in the long run.

The second step for handling stressful interactions is to use a diversion – if required. A diversion could be taking a brisk walk, deep breathing, listening to music, or engaging in some routine task. This helps block negative tendencies to dwell on the situation. It also prevents you from exaggerating the problem further or becoming even more stressed. A diversion also creates some distance between you and the stressful situation, and gives you space to calmly work out your response.

Remember Gail? She has identified her tendency to challenge the client in frustration. Gail has now decided she needs a distraction to calm her when she feels frustrated with the client.

Gail remembers the deep breathing technique she learned in her yoga classes. She decides that, prior to the next potentially stressful call with the client, she'll take a walk and engage in the breathing exercise to calm herself.

Exercise - Reverting Attention to Work

What do you think are the benefits of diverting your attention from a negative interpersonal situation at work?

Options:

1 - It puts some distance between you and the situation so you can view it more objectively.

2 - It counteracts the temptation to exaggerate the problem.

3 - It allows you to focus on what you're there for – work.

4 - It gives the other person time to realize that you're right.

Answer:

Option 1: This option is correct. Using a diversion, such as deep breathing techniques, allows you to focus and view the situation clearly.

Option 2: This option is correct. A diversion, such as a brisk walk, can give you the time required to see the situation in perspective.

Option 3: This option is incorrect. A large part of our work entails interacting with others. Therefore, interpersonal issues must be addressed.

Option 4: This option is incorrect. A diversion gives you time to think about the situation more objectively. You may come to the conclusion that you were wrong.

Correct answer(s):

1 - It puts some distance between you and the situation so you can view it more objectively.

2 - It counteracts the temptation to exaggerate the problem.

Replacing Negative Thoughts

The third step for handling stressful interactions is to replace negative thoughts with positive thoughts. To do

165

this, you must identify how your reactions to stress can cause distortions in your thinking, perceptions, or attitudes.

Typical thought distortions include overgeneralization, unwarranted magnification of issues, attributing blame, mind-reading, or adopting black-and-white thinking.

Overgeneralization

Overgeneralization is grouping similar experiences together and deciding that all such experiences will have the same outcome. For instance, if you had a bad experience with your first manager, you may have a mistrust of future managers.

Magnification

Magnification is exaggerating the significance of a negative event. For example, you find you've made a relatively minor error, and assume you'll be fired.

Blame

Blame is inappropriately holding others responsible, or considering someone guilty. For example, you could focus too much on finding scapegoats for an error, rather than on finding a solution.

Mind-reading

Mind-reading is assuming you know what people are thinking, even if their actions are neutral or indicate the opposite. For instance, people who frequently butt in or finish someone's sentence are assuming they know what's going to be said.

Black-and-white thinking

Black-and-white thinking is having an all-or-nothing attitude. Perfectionists often engage in this type of thinking. For example, believing if you can't complete a task a certain way, then don't do it at all.

Focus on Positive Thoughts

Once you've identified your negative thoughts, replace them with positive ones. A good place to start is to question these thoughts. Ask yourself whether there's any evidence to support your assumptions.

Then next step is to replace these thoughts with more realistic, beneficial thoughts by removing your automatic thought responses. For example, you could think, "This person isn't really talking too much. It's my own impatience that's causing me to feel frustrated."

During your interactions, take time to actively listen. Maintain good eye contact and avoid interrupting the person. Instead, interrupt your own inner dialog and focus on the other person. You'll get more information, improve the quality of your reactions, and view the situation more objectively.

Remember Gail? She has identified her tendency to challenge the client in frustration and used a diversion to manage her reactions effectively. Gail's now questioning why she becomes so frustrated with the client.

She realizes that, because she's a perfectionist, she's uncomfortable with changing goals and deadlines. She wants to get the job done right, and therefore doesn't like tight deadlines. This is an example of black-and-white thinking.

Gail now realizes that replacing negative thoughts with positive thoughts helped her to clarify her perception of the situation. She realized that she exaggerated the amount of changes requested from the client. The more emotionally involved she was, the more likely she'd have a distorted view of the situation.

Automatic negative thoughts can be replaced by remaining calm and putting yourself in the other person's shoes, or thinking about how someone you respect might react in your situation.

Exercise - Positive Thought Patterns

Which of these statements are examples of replacing negative thought patterns with positive thought patterns?

Options:

1 - "I misunderstood. He was only trying to ensure my success with the project."

2 - "She must be really under pressure to lash out like that."

3 - "I can't believe I didn't see it before. She's lazy and I should address the issue with her manager."

4 - "That explains it. She was only looking out for herself."

5 - "He didn't say my performance was poor overall. He just queried an item in my report."

Answer:

Option 1: This option is correct. Reflecting on someone's positive intentions is an example of replacing negative thought patterns with positive ones.

Option 2: This option is correct. Thinking about a colleague's pressured circumstances is an example of replacing negative thought patterns with positive ones.

Option 3: This option is incorrect. Blaming a colleague for being lazy isn't an example of replacing negative thought patterns with positive ones.

Option 4: This option is incorrect. Assuming a colleague is self-centered isn't an example of replacing negative thought patterns with positive ones.

Option 5: This option is correct. Having objective evidence for your negative thought can help you replace it with a more positive thought.

Correct answer(s):

1 - "I misunderstood. He was only trying to ensure my success with the project."

2 - "She must be really under pressure to lash out like that."

5 - "He didn't say my performance was poor overall. He just queried an item in my report."

The final step for handling stressful interactions is to prepare to interact positively. If you let yourself get into a negative frame of mind about an interaction, that interaction is much less likely to be successful. Start by clarifying what's emotionally challenging about the interaction. For example, if you're unable to complete a task, you may be afraid that your manager will become irritable.

Success Conditions

Begin by replacing negative thoughts with positive ones. Then determine what you need to succeed. For example, you may need information from your manager rather than from a report. Ideally, write down what you need, as this can help to clarify the details in your mind. You can then examine the pros and cons of different possible approaches. By clarifying the outcome you need, you're much more likely to get it.

Next, choose the right communication. It could be in person, by telephone, or by e-mail depending on what's appropriate for your needs. Person-to-person communication is best for sensitive matters. Telephone conversations are appropriate when physical distance is an issue.

E–mail communication is ideal if you've written out your thoughts, and it helps avoid misunderstandings. Take time to ensure the e-mail is professional, void of emotion, and that each sentence is relevant.

When interacting in person, you'll be more successful if you show empathy. Consider how your approach will make the other person feel and how she is likely to react and why. Put yourself in her shoes and verbalize her possible responses.

Exercise - Benefits of Being Prepared

What are the benefits of appropriately preparing for a potentially stressful interaction?

Options:

1 - Being able to monitor your feelings and tendencies can help you become self-aware. This helps you prevent adverse future automatic responses.

2 - Using diversions can help distract you from a negative thought pattern such as over-analyzing the situation.

3 - Replacing negative thoughts with positive thoughts helps you gain an objective, rather than subjective, view of interactions with colleagues.

4 - Working relationships are by nature unpredictable. Being adequately prepared for the stressful interaction makes sure you're the winner.

5 - You can control your own behavior, but not the behavior of others. Therefore, you should visualize all outcomes, including the worst-case scenario.

Answer:

Option 1: This option is correct. Becoming aware of your own emotions helps you avoid automatic unhelpful responses to the pressure of the interaction.

Option 2: This option is correct. Diversion can help you avoid obsessing about the situation and exaggerating the problem, which are likely to make the interaction more tense.

Option 3: This option is correct. The process of replacing thoughts is essential if you're to avoid letting emotions cloud your view of the situation.

Option 4: This option is incorrect. Clarifying the positive outcome you want to achieve from an interaction makes it much more likely you'll achieve a positive outcome.

Option 5: This option is incorrect. If you allow yourself to get into a negative frame of mind about the interaction, you make it more likely that it will be negative.

Correct answer(s):

1 - Being able to monitor your feelings and tendencies can help you become self-aware. This helps you prevent adverse future automatic responses.

2 - Using diversions can help distract you from a negative thought pattern such as over-analyzing the situation.

3 - Replacing negative thoughts with positive thoughts helps you gain an objective, rather than subjective, view of interactions with colleagues.

Exercise - A Difficult Clients

You're bracing for a stressful interaction with a difficult client. Select the actions in the correct order.

Options:

A - Ask yourself what the likely outcome would be to challenging a difficult client.

B - Distract yourself by talking to a colleague about a different issue.

C - Question if the client's really difficult or within his rights to demand the highest standard.

D - Decide in this case it would be best to meet the client face-to-face.

Answer:

Ask yourself what the likely outcome would be to challenging a difficult client is ranked the first step. This is an example of understanding the implications of negative reactions. This is an action you can take when monitoring your feelings and tendencies to react negatively to pressure situations.

Distract yourself by talking to a colleague about a different issue is ranked the second step. This is an example of using a diversion to avoid exaggerating the problem further. This helps block any negative tendencies to dwell on the issue.

Question if the client's really difficult or within his rights to demand the highest standard is ranked the third step. This is an example of the process of replacing negative thoughts with positive thoughts. This helps clarify your perception of the situation.

Decide in this case it would be best to meet the client face-to-face is ranked the fourth step. This is an example of choosing an appropriate means of communication while preparing to interact positively.

To Conclude

There are circumstances in the workplace where interactions with colleagues can generate pressure.

Reacting negatively to colleagues in pressure situations can be damaging to work relationships.

A four-step technique can help you handle stressful interactions. First, monitor your feelings and tendencies toward instinctive or automatic responses. Then use a diversion to avoid being dominated by negative thoughts. Next, replace negative and distorted thoughts with positive thoughts. Finally, prepare to interact positively.

CHAPTER SIX

Conclusion

There are three simple strategies to achieve performance under pressure:
1. develop the right attitude for performance under pressure,
2. take action for performance under pressure, and
3. achieve relational performance under pressure.

There are two main principles to help you control your reaction to pressure. First, you take control of yourself by taking stock of your emotions, establishing a sense of calm, accepting that you can't control everything, and using self-talk. Second, you cultivate a "success mentality" by using your emotions to your advantage, boosting self-confidence, having a "go to" statement prepared, focusing on what you can achieve, and adopting an attitude that's conducive to success.

Stressful situations tend to distort how a situation is perceived. And, you need discipline to see the real picture. Discipline and one simple four steps strategy that you can follow to optimize your perception of situations.

First, notice and understand your automatic thoughts. These thoughts often arise from emotional reactions to situations and may go undetected at first. Second, identify thought distortions. Common types of thought distortions include having a negative bias, blame, emotive reasoning, and exaggeration.

The third step is to question whether there is any evidence for this kind of thinking. The fourth step is to revise your thoughts. This involves restating them in a more positive way, by separating them from any emotional or automatic thinking. And, I do agree, it sounds difficult the first time. But, with time this will become just another good behavior that you exhibit.

The four work styles are expressives, drivers, amiables, and analysts. Under pressure, expressives can go on the offensive, drivers can become dictatorial, amiables may become acquiescent, and analysts may become excessively detached from others. There are circumstances in the workplace where interactions with colleagues can generate pressure. Reacting negatively to colleagues in pressure situations can be damaging to work relationships.

And here also you will learn a four-step technique that can help you handle stressful interactions. First, monitor your feelings and tendencies toward instinctive or automatic responses. Then use a diversion to avoid being dominated by negative thoughts. Next, replace negative and distorted thoughts with positive thoughts. Finally, prepare to interact positively.

***